BASIC CONCEPTS
OF
ECONOMICS

Dr. Surender Ahlawat

Dedicated to

Almighty God

Preface

Economic analysis has gained an important position in every field of life around the world. The base of every activity of life is economics. The application of economic tools and techniques not only reveals the pattern of economic variables but helps in arriving at optimum solution to the problem. Application of economic tools for economic analysis has become inevitable today.

This book is a modest attempt to bring the various basic concepts of economics in a simple and clear fashion. I have taken a great care to illustrate each point with suitable example. Figures and tables are used throughout for facilitating discussion.

The basic aim of this book is to create an interest in economics in the minds of all readers. Various basic aspects of economics are presented in a scientific manner with adopting the basic approach of questioning. The books covers the topics - Economics- An Introduction; Basic Economic Problems; Basic Units of Economic Analysis; Economic Systems; Economic Institutions; National Income Accounting; Saving and Investment; Demand and

Supply; Elasticity; Utility; Production; Cost and Revenue; Market; Income Distribution; Entrepreneurs; Money; Monetary Policy; Inflation; Business Cycle; Employment and Unemployment; International Trade; Exchange Rate; Budgeting; Public Expenditure, Revenue, Debt and Taxes; Fiscal policy; Banking; Central Bank and Financial Institutions.

However this endeavor of our have been successful would be known by the response the book receives from the readers and appreciation from the learned teachers. I would always gratefully welcome their valuable suggestions and observations to improve the book.

In completing this book, above all, I bow my head before the 'God' without whose blessings my present book would not have been possible in the present existed form and thanks for giving me patience and strength to overcome difficulties, which crossed my way in the accomplishment of this endeavor. I gratefully acknowledge the help of my wife Dr. Rachna Ahlawat for her help and support in preparing this book. I also place on record my deep sense of gratitude to my publishers   for their wholehearted cooperation all through the process of production of this book.

(Surender Ahlawat)

Contents

4

14

Chapter: 1

Economics- An Introduction

1.1 Introduction

The term Economics has been taken by two Greek language words: Oikos (Household0 and Nemein (Management). Thus they mean management of household. **Economics is a social science which deals with human wants and their satisfaction.** It is mainly concerned with the way in which a society chooses to employ its scarce resources which have alternative uses, for the production of goods for present and future consumption. Political economy is another name for economics. "Polis" in Greek means a State. The early writers used the term "Political Economy" for the management of the State. A person who runs a family is expected to make the best use of the income of the household. Similarly, the State is expected to get the maximum benefit for the society. We study economics because there is scarcity of many goods we want. This problem is common to the individual as well as the State. That is why we say

6

Economics is the science of scarcity. And scarcity is the basic fact of life. Our wants are unlimited but means are limited. This leads to choice making. If there is unlimited supply of goods which satisfy our wants, the problem of choice will not arise. It is true that we have many wants. But all wants are not of equal importance. So we choose the more important and the more urgent wants. So choice is the essence of economic activity. We may also say that economics is the science of choice. Of course, all goods we want are not scarce. There are certain things like air and sunshine which are available in abundance. Though they are very essential for our life, we do not pay any price for them. They are free goods and they are not very important for our study. But many things we want are scarce and we have to pay a price for them. So, in economics, we study how prices of different things are determined. We may also say that economics is a science that deals with pricing process.

1.2 Definitions of Economics

As you look on your study of economics, you will study the comment that there are as many definitions of economics as there are economists. Here are some of the great thinkers in this field had to say about the subject matter of economics and their definitions can be divided into the following categories:

1.2.1 Adam Smith's Definition (Wealth Definition)

Adam Smith (1723-90) defined economics in his famous book "Wealth of Nations" (1776) as follows: "*Economics is an enquiry into the nature and causes of wealth of nations*". He is known as the Father of Economics because he was the first person who put all the economic ideas in a systematic way.

Criticism: A great demerit of Adam Smith's definition is that there is overemphasis on wealth. There is no doubt that we have to study about wealth in economics. But it can be only a part of the study. There is the other side. In fact, it is a more important side and that is the study of man. Economics is a social science. Hence the proper study of mankind should be man and not wealth alone. So this definition is not a precise definition.

1.2.2 Alfred Marshall's Definition (Welfare Definition)

Alfred Marshall (1842-1924) wrote a book "Principles of Economic" in 1890. In it, he defined economics as *"Economics is a study of mankind in the ordinary business of life. It examines that part of individual and social action which is most closely connected with the attainment and use of material requisites of well being"*.

Criticism: The definition of Marshall has been strongly criticized by Lionel Robbins. He says that Marshall's definition misrepresents the science of economics. If we go by the definition of Marshall. In economics we should consider only those activities which promote material welfare. But many activities do not promote welfare but are rightly considered as economic activity.

1.2.3 Lord Lionel Robbins' definition (Scarcity Definition)

Lord Lionel Robbins has defined economics in his book "An Essay on the Nature and significance of Economic Science" as follows: *"Economics is a science that studies human behavior as a relationship between ends and scarce means which have alternative uses".*

Criticism: The demerit of Robbins' definition is that it makes economics a scientific study. Ethical aspects of economic problems are not taken into account in discussions. In other words, the moral aspects are not considered. And it does not try to establish a link between economics and welfare. But some economists criticize this view. They say that as economics is a social science, its aim should be promotion of human welfare. That is why some economists say Robbins' definition has no human touch about it. It looks at economics only as the science of

pricing process. But economics is more than a theory of value or resource allocation.

1.2.4 Samuelson's Definition (Modern Definition of Economics)

Samuelson's definition is known as a modern definition of economics. According to Samuelson, *"Economics is a social science concerned chiefly with the way society chooses to employ its resources, which have alternative uses, to produce goods and services for present and future consumption".*

The above definition is general in nature. There are many common points in the definitions of Robbins and Samuelson. Samuelson's definition tells us that economics is a social science and it is mainly concerned with the way how society employs its limited resources for alternative uses. All this we find in the definition of Robbins. But Samuelson goes a step further and discusses how a society uses limited resources for producing goods and services for present and future consumption of various people or groups. An interesting point that Samuelson tells is that the society may or may not make use of money.

The above definitions of economics have one shortcoming or the other. So we have to make a proper synthesis of these definitions to draw the meaning of economics based on these definitions which is as follow:

Economics is a social science. It deals with human behavior in society. Therefore, we can say that economics is a social science that deals with:

- ✓ The creation of wealth from scarce resources;
- ✓ The production and distribution of goods and services for consumption;
- ✓ The behavior, interaction and well-being of the groups involved in the above activities;
- ✓ The fact that there is a trade-off involved in production and in consumption.

1.3 Nature of Economics

Nature of Economics refers to whether is a science or an art or both. The next question is that if it is science, is it a positive science or normative science or both.

1.3.1 Economics as a science

Science may be defined as a systematized body of knowledge concerning the relationship between causes and effects of a particular phenomenon. Just as physics and chemistry are sciences, economics is also a science. We observe facts, conduct experiments

10

and make generalizations in physics and chemistry after testing the results. The same scientific methods are followed in economics also. Economics, like all other sciences, studies the relationship between cause and effect. Sciences may be broadly divided into physical sciences and social sciences. Physics and chemistry are examples of physical sciences. Economics is a social science. It studies about an economic aspect of human behavior. And human behavior is full of complexity. It is not easy to study it. So economic science is not as precise and exact as the physical sciences. But economics has a greater right to be considered as a science than other social sciences like politics or history because in economics we make use of money as a measuring unit of utility.

1.3.2 Economics: positive or normative science?

After proving economics as a science, the next question is whether it is positive or normative science or both. Positive Science can be defined as a body of systematized knowledge concerning what is, while normative science tries to develop criteria for what ought to be" Positive economics is mainly concerned with the description of economic events and it tries to formulate theories to explain them. But in normative economics, we give more importance to ethical judgments. Normative economics is concerned with the ideal rather than the actual situations. Statements on economics may be classified into positive statements and normative statements. If there is disagreement over a statement, we can find out whether it is true or false by verifying facts. But when there is disagreement over a normative statement, we cannot settle the issue simply by appealing to facts. The questions, "what are the policies that the Government should follow to reduce unemployment? What should it do to reduce inflation? Are all questions in positive economics? On the other hand, if we ask the question, "should the government be more concerned about unemployment than inflation?", then it is a normative one.

1.3.3 Economics as an Art

Whether economics is an Art? This is also a controversial question among the economists. Robbins, Walras, etc. do not consider economics to be an art. However, Marshall, Piggu, etc. are of the opinion that economics is an art. In this way, some are in favour of it and another are against of this statement. So it is very essential to know what an art is. Art is defined as a practical application of knowledge for achieving definite ends. As an art, economics helps the people in the solution of their practical problems.

From the above discussion, it can be well said that economics is both a science as well as an art and it is truly a social science.

1.4 Scope of Economics

Scope of economics refers to what is and what is not studied in economics. Under scope of economics, we study the subject matter of economics. Subject matter of economics is dynamic and growing with the passage of time. It is the description of nature and behaviour of an economy and economic system to investigate the economic problems with the objective of offering solutions. In the subject matter of economics, we include economic activities like production, consumption, investment, exchange, product and factor pricing, economic system like capitalism, socialism and mixed economy, economic policies like monetary, fiscal policies etc and application of economics in agriculture, industry, labour and environment etc.

1.5 Importance of Economics

Now Economics is considered as one of the important branches of social sciences. It is of great practical value in our daily life. In economics, we study the subject not only to know the truth for its own sake, but to find out a way for many economic and social problems of the society. "Knowledge for the sake of knowledge" is not the goal of an economist. Economics must be fruit-bearing subject. Of course, an economist has no readymade answer for immediate problems. But he can help the Government in making broad economic policies. According to Keynes, "the theory of economics does not furnish a body of settled conclusions immediately applicable to policy. It is a method, rather than a doctrine, an apparatus of the mind, a technique of thinking, which helps its possessor to draw correct conclusions". Most of the problems of the modern State are economic in nature. So economists play an important role in the affairs of the State. During World War II, the German economy was damaged heavily. There was inflation, shortage of goods and mass unemployment. But the German economy recovered quickly by following the advice of an economist Ludwig Erhard. The German recovery is considered an economic miracle. Similarly, Keynes had great influence on the economic policies of the American government when it was in great economic trouble during the 1930s. In economics, we study about things like prices, rent, wages, interest, profits and taxation. All these affect every person one way or the other. It has been rightly said, "You cannot be in any real sense a citizen, unless you are also in some degree an economist".

1.6 Limitation of Economics

The above discussion is incomplete if we do not have the knowledge about the limitations of the study of economics. The main limitations of economics are given as:

- ✓ Economics studies only human activities only.
- ✓ Economics theories are not exact and universal as the law of natural sciences.
- ✓ Economics theories are based on some certain assumption.
- ✓ Economics study only rational man.
- ✓ The definition and subject matter of economics is very controversial.

Review of Questions

1.   State and examine the criticism against various definitions of Economics.
2.   Is economics a positive science or a normative science?
3.   Discuss the nature and scope of economics.
4.   Explain the importance and limitations of economics.

Chapter: 2

Basic Economic Problems

2.1 Economic Problem

Every country has some central economic problems. Before go further deep in the study, it is necessary to know what is meant by economic problems. An economic problem indicates to that problem which is concerned with the optimum allocation of the present resources and with the growth and distribution of future resources. In others words, economic problem is a problem of choice of economizing the use of resources. Further it is also important to know about choice. Choice is the art of selecting among restricted alternatives whereas economizing is making the best use of resource available. Sometimes Economics is called the science of choice making. Choices can be made at the personal level or at the national level. The existence of limited resources and the different choices made at the personal level and national level results in economic problems. There are three basic reasons behind economic problems which are as follow:

- ✓ **Unlimited Wants:** Human wants are unlimited and these are multiplying day by days.
- ✓ **Scarcity of Resources:** Mostly resources on the earth are limited in nature especially manmade goods.
- ✓ **Resources have alternative uses:** Mostly resources on the earth have alternative uses.

Human wants are unlimited but resources, which satisfy these unlimited wants, are limited. So every economy has to make choice as how to make optimum use of limited resources which have alternative uses. Economics is the art and science of making choice under conditions of scarcity. What are the basic issues about which choices are to be made? Any society must make choices about three important problems. They are

2.1.1 What to produce and How much to produce?

The first problem of the economy is what goods and services be produced and how much to be produced. For example, what must be produced Food or weapons; if so, in what quantities?

2.1.2 How to produce?

Second problem of the economy is how to produce. This problem is concerned with the choice of technique. For example, whether electricity produces from thermal power or hydro power?

2.1.3 For whom to produce?

Third problem of the economy is for whom to produce. This problem is related to the distribution of the production. For example, whether goods should be produce for few rich and many poor or most people?

These three central problems of an economy are interdependent. The society must make proper choice about them in order to meet the development aspirations of people satisfactorily. The above three questions are common to all economies but every economic system attempts to make its own choice. The nature of a particular choice in a particular society depends on its specific economic system.

Another important question about the basic economic problems is: How do we make choice in an economy? At the individual level you must choose among alternatives like, - whether to watch cricket highlights in T.V. or study for another extra hour. It is important to note that choices are made due to scarcity. If there is no scarcity, there would be no need to choose. Similarly as choice must be made from alternatives, it involves comparison of cost and benefit.

2.2. Opportunity Cost

When you choose a particular alternative, the next best alternative must be given up. For example, if you choose to watch cricket highlights in T.V., you must give up an extra hour study. The choice of watching cricket in T.V. results in the loss of the next best alternative an extra hour study instead. Thus by watching T.V., you have forgone the opportunity of scoring an extra five or ten marks in examination. Thus the "opportunity cost" is the cost of something in terms of an opportunity forgone (and the benefits that could be received from that opportunity). In other words, the opportunity cost of an action is the value of next best alternative forgone. The consideration of opportunity costs is one of the key differences between the concepts of 'economic cost' and 'accounting cost'. Choices are mostly made on the basis of opportunity cost.

2.3 Production Possibility Curve

Like the individuals, a society as whole has limited resources. It has to decide what to produce with the limited resource. It has to make choice about the quantity of different commodities. Choice emanates from scarcity. Thus our choice is always constrained or limited by scarcity of our resources. Suppose we have enough resources we can produce all that we want. All such choices can be made with help of production possibility curve. The production-possibility curve separates outcomes that are possible for the society to produce from those which cannot be produced subject to the available resources. Let us consider an economy with only so many people, so many industries, so much of electricity and natural resources in deciding what shall be produced and how these resources are to be allocated among thousands of different possible commodities. How many industries are to produce steel? How much electricity to be provided for agriculture; how much for industries?. Whether to provide free electricity to farmer or not? These problems are complicated. Therefore, to simplify let us assume there are only two goods to be produced - apples and oranges. Production Possibility Quantity of Apples Quantity of Oranges Schedule Possibilities

Table 2.1: Production Possibility Schedule

Production possibilities	Quantity of Apples	Quantity of Oranges
A	4	0
B	3	2
C	2	4
D	1	6
E	0	8

In the above table, A and E are possibilities where the economy either produces 100 percent of apples or 100 percent of oranges alone. But the production possibility curve assumes the production of two goods in different combinations. Possibilities A, B,C ,D and E are such that the economy produces 4 units of apples and 0 units of oranges in possibility A, 3 units of apples and 2 units of orange in possibility B, 2 units of apples and 4 units of oranges in possibility C, 1 unit of apple and 6 units of oranges in possibility D, 0 unit of apples and 8 units of oranges in possibility E. Thus we see that if we are willing to have more of oranges, we should be willing to sacrifice more of apples. For instance, to reach possibility C from B, the economy produces 2 units more of oranges by sacrificing 1 unit of apples. A full employment economy must always in producing one good be giving up something of another. This assumes of course, that at least some resources can be transferred from one good to another. Such choice of one particular alternative involves opportunity cost of foregoing the other. Hence, the decisions of the society will be based on the comparison of costs and benefits of each alternative. In doing so, both the monetary and social cost and benefit should be the basis of any choice.

Figure1: Production Possibility Curve

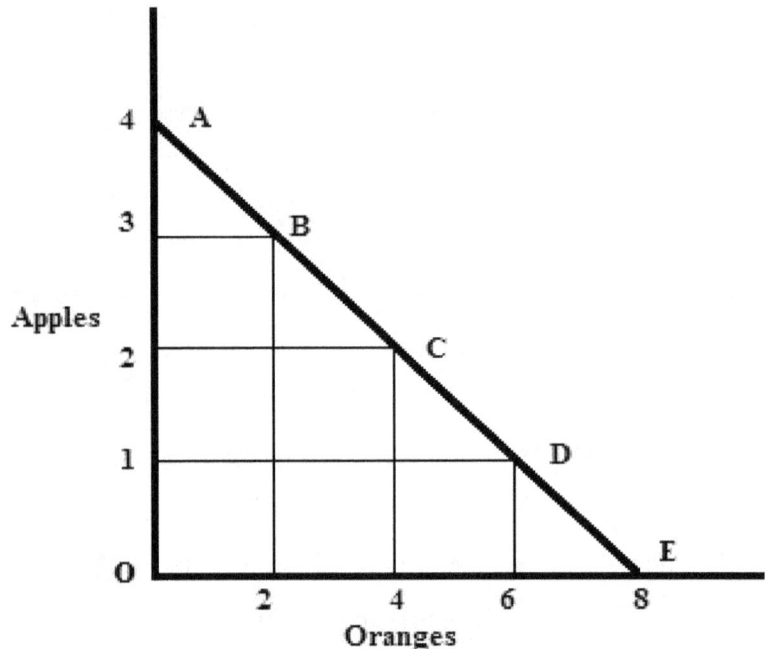

Thus the one that gives the maximum benefit at minimum cost to the whole society should be the best choice. We can picture the production possibility schedule by drawing a smooth curve (Figure 1). Units of oranges are measured horizontally and that of apples on the vertical axis. The curve A and E depict the various possible combinations of the two goods - A, B, C, D, and E. Thus a list of all the possible combinations of apples and oranges makes up production possibilities. The production possibility curve is also known as transformation curve or production possibility frontier. This curve shows the rate of transformation of one product into the

20

other when the economy moves from one possibility point to the other. All possible combinations lying on the production possibility curve show the combinations of the two goods that can be produced by the existing resources. Any combination lying inside the production curve such as U in the figure indicates that resources are not being fully employed in the best-known way. Any point outside the production possibility frontier, such as L implies that the economy does not have adequate resources to produce this combination. But a shift outside the production possibility frontier certainly indicates economic development. This is possible by technological advancement and increase in supply of factors of production.

Review of Questions

1. What is opportunity cost?
2. Define choice?
3. Define Economic problems.
4. Explain the basic problems of an Economy.
5. Describe the 'production possibility curve' with a suitable diagram.

Chapter: 3

Basic Units of Economic Analysis

Economic units are those units which determine the different economic activities like consumption, production, exchange, etc and all these economic activities are called basic units of economy. Before go further, it is important to know about meaning of economy.

3.1 The economy

Economics recognizes that resources are scarce. The economy is the mechanism through which these scarce resources are organized for the production of goods and services. These goods and services satisfy the needs and wants of the different groups in the economy. The three main groups in the economy are households, firms and the government. They are also known as types of economic activities.

3.1.1 Household

A household is one decision-making unit. In economics, two

assumptions are made about households. First, households consume goods and services. Second, households are the owners of the factors of production. A factor of production (factor input) is any resource used to produce goods and services. The four factors of production are land, labour, capital and entrepreneurship.

3.1.2 Firms

A firm is also a decision-making unit. This is the unit that produces goods and services. To produce these goods and services, firms buy factor services from households.

3.3.1.3 Government

The government provides the framework of rules and laws for households and firms to operate within; in some economies, the government is also involved in production.

3.2 Main Divisions of Economics

There are four main divisions of economics. They are consumption, production, exchange and distribution. In modern times, economists add one more division and that is public finance. In public finance, we study about the economics of government. The economic functions of the modern State have increased to a great extent. So, public finance has become an important branch of economics. All the above divisions are interrelated. And they are dependent on each other.

3.2.1 Consumption

Consumption deals with the satisfaction of human wants. There is economic activity in the world because there are wants. When a want is satisfied, the process is known as consumption.

Generally, in plain language, when we use the term "consumption", what we mean is usage. But in economics, it has a special meaning. We can speak of the consumption of the services of a lawyer, just as we speak of the consumption of food. In the sub-division dealing with consumption, we study about the nature of wants, the classification of wants and some of the laws dealing with consumption such as the law of diminishing marginal utility, Engel's law of family expenditure and the law of demand.

3.2.2 Production

Production refers to the creation of wealth. Strictly speaking, it refers to the creation of utilities. And utility refers to the ability of a good to satisfy a want. There are three kinds of utility. They are form utility, place utility and time utility. Production refers to all activities which are undertaken to produce goods which satisfy human wants. Land, labour, capital and organization are the four factors of production. In the subdivision dealing with production, we study about the laws which govern the factors of production. They include Malthusian Theory of population and the laws of returns. We also study about the localization of industries and industrial organization.

3.2.3 Exchange

In modern times, no one person or country can be self-sufficient. This gives rise to exchange. In exchange, we give one thing and take another. Goods may be exchanged for goods or for money. If goods are exchanged for goods, we call it barter. Modern economy is a money economy. As goods are exchanged for money, we study in economics about the functions of money, the role of banks and we also study how prices are determined. We also discuss various aspects of international trade.

3.2.4 Distribution

Wealth is produced by the combination of land, labour, capital and organization. And it is distributed in the form rent, wages, interest and profits. In economics, we are not much interested in personal distribution. That is, we do not analyze how it is distributed among different persons in the society. But we are interested in functional distribution. As the four factors or agents of production perform different functions in production, we have to reward them.

3.2.5 Public Finance

Public finance deals with the economics of government. It studies mainly about the income and expenditure of government. So we have to study about different aspects relating to taxation, public expenditure, and public debt and so on.

We may note that the subject of economics is divided into consumption, production, exchange, distribution, and public finance only for the sake of convenience. We should not look at it in a rigid way. We must not consider them as watertight compartments. They are related to each other and they are interdependent also. For example, we cannot have consumption without production. The aim of production is creation of wealth. And we produce wealth not for its own sake but for the satisfaction of human wants. In other words, we produce goods because we want them for consumption. So the

25

ultimate aim of production is promotion of human welfare. Production is means and consumption is the end. Generally, people produce goods for market. So exchange takes place. Exchange is the connecting link between production and consumption. The economic welfare of people in a nation depends on how wealth is produced and on how it is distributed. If there is no proper distribution, it will result in inequalities of income and wealth. This, in turn, will affect consumption and production. So we find that all the divisions of economics are interrelated and interdependent.

3.3 Static and dynamic concepts

Time element is very useful in studying the working of an economy. There are two main lines of approach. They are 1. Static analysis and 2. Dynamic analysis. In the case of static analysis, we examine a problem at any given moment of time. Even in static analysis, sometimes we consider a short period rather than a single point. We assume that some changes take place during the short period. The method of approach where we take note of changes in the short period is known as comparative statics. For example, in *comparative statics*, we compare the state of economy at one moment to the state of the economy at another moment. Marshall's analysis of supply and demand is a good example of comparative statics. In dynamic analysis, we examine the path or process by which the economy moves from one state of equilibrium to another. Time element is an important factor is dynamic analysis. Change is the key word in dynamic analysis. For example, investment during a period may depend upon the rate of interest in the previous period.

The study of the trade cycle may be given as a good example of dynamic analysis.

3.4 Stocks and flows

Stocks and flows are basic concepts in economics. Stocks can be measured at a given point of time. A flow is a quantity that can be measured only in terms of a specified period of time. In other words, it has a time dimension. For example, wealth is a stock and income is a flow.

3.5 Micro economics and macro economics

Economic theory can be broadly divided into *micro economics* and *macroeconomics*. The term *micro* means small and *macro* means large. In microeconomics, we deal with problems such as the output of a single firm or industry, price of a single commodity and spending on goods by a single household. Macroeconomics studies the economic system as a whole. In it, we get a complete picture of the working of the economy. It is a study of the relations between broad economic aggregates such as total employment, saving and investment. We may also say that macro economics is the theory of income, employment, prices and money. That is why macroeconomics is sometimes studied under the title "Income and Employment Analysis".

3.6 Economic Laws

Like other social sciences, economics has its own laws. A law is a statement of what must happen given certain conditions. Every cause has a tendency to produce some result. For example, in Physics, we study that things fall to the ground because of gravitation. The law of gravitation is a statement of tendency. Similarly, the laws of economics are statements of tendencies. For example, according to the law of demand, when there is fall in the price of a good, the demand for it will expand. It means that there is a tendency among people to buy more

when there is fall in the price of a good. Similarly, if price rises, they will buy less. Laws operate under certain conditions. If these conditions change, they will not operate. This is applicable to all sciences. When some economic laws do not operate, it means that the conditions have changed. We may broadly classify sciences into physical sciences and social sciences. Physics and chemistry are examples of physical sciences. Economics, politics are examples of social sciences. The laws of physical sciences are exact. But the laws of economics are not as exact as the laws of physical sciences. For example, we have the law of gravitation. It is a simple and exact statement. But in economics, we deal with human beings and their behavior with reference to economic activity. We cannot conduct experiments with human beings either within the laboratory or outside it. That is why economic laws cannot be as exact as the laws of physical sciences. We may also note that we study about average human behavior in economics. As economics deals with man and his behavior, its laws are complex and inexact. That is why Marshall has said that "the laws of economics are to be compared with the laws of tides rather than with the simple and exact law of gravitation". The science of tides explains the tides rise and fall under the influence of the Sun and the Moon. Probably there will be high tide on a full moon night. It may be there or it may not be there. It is only a probability. Similarly, economic laws also indicate probable trends. For example, when there is increase in the quantity of money, there may be increase in the price level. But we cannot say exactly by how much prices will rise. But economic laws are more exact than the laws of history and politics because economics make use of money as a measuring rod of utility. Though money is a rough measure, it gives a concrete shape to economic laws.

All economic laws are based on certain assumptions. Let us take the law of demand. It tells that "other things being equal", when the price of a good falls, people will buy more of the good. By "other things are equal" we mean (1) that the income of the people remains the same, (2) that their tastes remain the same (3) that the prices of other goods remain the same, and (4) that no new substitute for the good is discovered. The law will hold good only when the above assumptions are fulfilled. Sometimes, it is said that the laws of economics are hypothetical. That is, we make an hypothesis. Only after it is verified by facts and experiments and found true, it becomes a law. But many economic laws cannot be verified by experiment. That is why we say sometimes that economic laws are hypothetical. The laws of physical sciences have universal application. But that is not generally the case with regard to economic laws. Of course, there are one or two exceptions. The Law of Diminishing Returns has universal application.

3.7 Importance of Economic Laws

Economic laws are of great importance in practical life.

29

Some economic laws are applicable to all types of economic systems. They have universal application. For example, we have the law of Diminishing Returns. There are other important laws such as the law of diminishing marginal utility and the law of demand. Some economists believe that the quantity theory of money is valid under all economic systems – capitalism or socialism or mixed economy. Let us take some important laws like the law of diminishing marginal utility, the law of demand, the law of diminishing returns and the Malthusian Theory of population and discuss their significance. The law of diminishing utility is based on actual experience. It tells that the more and more of a thing you have, the less and less you want it. It explains the relationship between the price of a good and the satisfaction you get from it. During summer, generally, there will be fall in the price of mangoes because they are available in plenty. So there is diminishing utility. And as price is related to marginal utility, the price falls. Progressive taxation is based on the law of diminishing utility. As the income increases, the Government ask the rich to pay more taxes by increasing the rates of taxation for them. For it believes that as a man gets more and more money, he will get diminishing utility from it. So even if he parts with more money, the sacrifice will not be much in his case.

The law of demand is based on actual experience. In practice we find that when price falls, demand increases. Price falls when supply is more. When there is increase in the supply of a good, its marginal utility diminishes. A seller will try to sell more of his good by reducing its price slightly. The law of diminishing marginal returns has universal application. In agriculture, it means that we cannot double the output by doubling labour and capital. The law applies to manufacturing industry also. The Malthusian theory of population tells that population increases

at a faster rate than food supply. It might not be an exact statement. But it was true in the case of most of the poor countries of the world until the Green Revolution. The Green Revolution helped in increasing agricultural productivity. There is the problem of over–population in most of the poor countries of the world. That is why they spend huge amounts on family planning to reduce population growth. So, most of the laws of economics are of great practical importance.

3.8 Basic Concepts

Every science has its own language. Economics has its own language. There are certain terms which are used in a special sense in economics. So we must understand the meaning of some basic concepts like wealth, goods, income, value, price and market. If we do not understand their meaning properly, it may result in a lot of confusion.

3.8.1 Wealth

In ordinary speech, when we refer to wealth, we mean money. But in economics, it has a special meaning. It refers to those scarce goods which satisfy our wants and which have money value. We may consider anything that has money value as wealth in economics. All economic goods have value–in–exchange. So wealth includes all economic goods. Wealth has been defined as *"stock of goods existing at a given time that have money value"*.

3.8.1.1 Characteristics of Wealth

The following are the characteristics of wealth:

- ✓ *It must possess utility*. It must have the power to satisfy a want. As Marshall says *"they must be desirable"*.
- ✓ *It must be limited in supply*. For example, air and sunshine are essential for life. We cannot live without them. But we do not consider them as wealth because they are available in large quantities. Such goods are known as free goods.
- ✓ *Wealth should be transferable*. That is, it should be possible for us to transfer the ownership from one person to another.
- ✓ *It must have money value*.
- ✓ *It may be external*. For example, the goodwill of a company is external wealth. Utility, scarcity and transferability are thus important characteristics of wealth.

3.8.1.2 Classification of Wealth

Wealth may be classified into a) personal wealth (individual wealth) b) social wealth (collective wealth), c) national wealth (a + b) and d) cosmopolitan wealth (e.g. ocean).

3.8.2 Goods

Anything that satisfies a human want can be considered as

"good" in economics, In economics, the term "goods" refer to material and non-material things. Just as an apple or a chair is a good, music or the services of actors, musicians and teachers are some of the examples of goods. Goods can be classified into *free goods and economic goods*. Goods like air and sunlight which are the gifts of nature are free goods. They are not scarce. So they do not command a price in the market. They are known as free goods. Economic goods command a price in the market. In other words, they have value-in-exchange. For, they are scarce in relation to demand. In this connection, we have to remember that what is a free good in one place can become an economic good in another place. It all depends on the supply of a good and the demand for it. For example, in some villages firewood is a free good. But in a town where we have to pay a price for it, it becomes an economic good. Similarly, water which is a free good becomes an economic good when there is scarcity of water. Goods may be further classified into

(1) consumers goods and

(2) Producers goods. Consumer's goods satisfy our wants directly. They can be classified into (1) perishable goods (eg. vegetables, fish and music) and (2) durable goods (eg. a house, a car, a radio). Capital goods satisfy our wants indirectly. Machines that are used to make machines are called capital goods. For example, car is a sort of machine. It is a consumers' good. But there must be some other machine to make a car. That machine is known as capital good or producer good. But what is a consumers' good in one place can become a producers' good in another place. For example, when

electricity is used for lighting purposes at home, it is a consumers' good. But the same electricity when used in factories for industrial purposes, it becomes a producers' good.

3.8.3 Income

In economics, when we refer to income, generally we mean money income. According to Seligman, "Income in the economic sense, is the flow of satisfactions from economic goods". We know that all economic goods form wealth. The main source of income is wealth. For example, if you own a house, it is your wealth. If you get rent from it, it is your income. There are two points about income – time and amount. There are two kinds of income – (1) money income and (2) Real Income. Generally people earn their incomes in the form of money. Money income is also known as nominal income. But the standard of living of people of a country depends on their real income. Real income depends upon the purchasing power of money and that in turn depends on the price level. Real income refers to the command of a person over actual commodities and services. Just because money incomes of people increase, we cannot say they are better off. It all depends upon how many goods they can command. Suppose, my money income is Rs. 10, and price of one kilo of rice is Rs. 10, then I can buy one kilo of rice or my income is worth of only one kilo of rice. In the next month, my money income is raised to Rs. 15, but the price of one kilo of rice is increased to Rs. 20. Now my income is worth only ¾ kilo of rice. Therefore, in spite of increase in money income, my real income has come down due to higher increase in price. *Real income is price adjusted money income.* National Income: National income refers to the value of commodities and services produced by a country during a year. Marshall defined national income as follows: "The labour and capital of country acting on its natural resources produce annually a certain net aggregate of commodities, material and immaterial, including services of all kinds. This is true net annual income or revenue of the country, or the national dividend". From the national income of a country, we can find out whether the country is rich or poor. And from the composition of national income, we can find out the relative importance of agriculture, industry and service sector in the economy. We get per capita income [(i.e) income per person per year] by dividing national income by the population of the country.

$$\text{Per capita income} = \frac{\text{National Income}}{\text{Population}} \quad \text{.... (1)}$$

3.8.4 Value

The term "value" refers to the exchange qualities of a good. According to Marshall, "the term value is relative and expresses the relation between two things at a particular place and time". Value is of two kinds (1) value–in–use and (2) value–in– exchange. Although air, rain and sunshine have value–in–use, they do not have value–in–exchange. In economics, we are interested only in those goods which have value–in–exchange. For a good to have value– in–exchange, it must possess utility, it must be scarce in relation to demand and it must be possible for us to exchange it. In other words, all economic goods have value-in-exchange. Value is generally measured in money and it is a relative term. The value of a thing changes according to time and situation. For example, ice has more value in summer than in winter.

3.8.5 Price

When value is expressed in money, it is called price. Generally, economists make no distinction between value and price. All prices are related to one another. They form the price system. The prices most familiar to us are the prices we pay for goods sold in market, that is, retail prices. Many payments like rent, wages and interest are also prices which we pay respectively to land, labour and capital. Price system plays a very important role in a capitalistic economy. Buyers express their desire for goods only through prices. Every price we pay for a good is a vote in favour of it. It is the price system that regulates the economic activity of a society.

3.8.6 Market

In the ordinary language, market refers to a place where goods are bought and sold. Thus Koyambedu market in Chennai refers to a place where vegetables are sold. In economics, market does not refer to any particular place in which goods are bought and sold. But it refers to buying and selling of a commodity. In a market a commodity is bought and sold under given conditions and there will be a number of buyers and sellers who will be in close touch with each other. For example, a fish market refers to buying and selling of fish; here both buyers and sellers are in close contact. According to Benham, "Market is any area over which the buyers and sellers are in close touch with one another either directly or through dealers, that price obtainable in one part of market affects the prices paid in other parts". Generally speaking, when we talk of markets, we refer to commodities that are bought and sold. But there are markets for thing sother than commodities. Thus there are labour markets, foreign exchange market, and capital market and so on. For example, we may say the market for an actor, say 'X', is dull. So there may be a market for anything which has a price.

3.8.1 Classification of Markets:

Markets may be classified according to space, time and the nature of competition. According to space, markets are classified into local market (eg. vegetables, flowers), national market (e.g. sarees) and international market (e.g. steel, cotton, sugar, tea). Markets can also be classified according to the type of competition. Thus, broadly we have perfect markets and imperfect markets. Markets can also be classified into short period markets and long period markets according to time. If the period is short, demand plays an important role in the market and if the period is longer, supply plays an important role. Thus markets can be classified according to space, time and the nature of competition that prevails.

Review of Questions

1. Distinguish between micro economics and macro economics.

2. Write a note on static and dynamic concepts.

3. Discuss the nature and importance of economics laws.

Chapter: 4

Economic Systems

4.1 Economic system

An economic system is a way of answering these basic questions. Different economic systems answer the above questions differently. An economic system refers to how the different economic elements will solve the central problems of an economy: what, how and for whom to produce. It refers to the production and distribution of goods and services within which economic activity takes place. It refers to the way different economic elements, individual workers and managers, productive organization such as factories or firms and government agencies are linked together to form an organic whole.

Economic system consists of various individuals and their institutions like banking institutions, educational institutions and economic institutions. The most general economic systems are:

✓ Traditional Economy

- ✓ Capitalist Economy
- ✓ Socialist Economy
- ✓ Mixed Economy

4.1.1 Traditional Economy

In traditional economy, the basic problems are solved by traditions and custom rules every aspect of behavior. It produces exactly to its consumption requirements. It is a subsistence economy. There are not much of sales as there is only small scale production. The same product will be produced by every generation. The production techniques are traditional.

4.1.2 Capitalist Economy

A capitalist economy is an economic system in which the production and distribution of commodities take place through the mechanism of free markets. Hence it is also called as market economy or free trade economy. Each individual be it a producer, consumer or resource owner has considerable economic freedom. An individual has the freedom to buy and sell any number of goods and services and to choose any occupation. Thus a market economy has no central coordinator guiding its operation. But self-organization emerges amidst the functioning of market forces namely supply, demand and price. The salient features of capitalism are

- ✓ **Right to Private Property:** Individuals have the right to buy and own property. There is no limit and they can own any amount of property. They also have legal rights to use their property in any way they like.

- ✓ **Profit-Motive:** Profit is the only motive for the functioning of capitalism. Production decisions involving high risks are taken by individual only to earn large profits. Hence, profit-motive is the basic force that drives the capitalist economy.

- ✓ **Freedom of Choice:** The question 'what to produce?' will be determined by the producers. They have the freedom to decide. The factors of production can also be employed anywhere freely to get due prices for their services. Similarly consumers have the freedom to buy anything they want.

- ✓ **Market Forces:** Market forces like demand, supply and price are the signals to direct the system. Most of the economic activities are centered on price mechanism. Production, consumption and distribution questions are expected to be solved by market forces.

- ✓ **Minimal Role of Government:** As most of the basic economic problems are expected to be solved by market forces, the government has minimal role in the economy. Their role will be limited to some important functions. They include regulation of market, defense, foreign policy, currency, etc.

4.1.2.1 Merits of Capitalist Economy

- ✓ **Increase in Productivity:** In a capitalist economy every farmer, trader or industrialist can hold property and use it in any way he likes. He increases the productivity to meet his own self-interest. This in turn leads to increase in income, saving and investment.

- ✓ **Maximizes the Welfare:** It is claimed that there is efficiency in production and resource use without any plan. The self-interest of individual also promotes society's welfare.

- ✓ **Flexible System:** The shortages and surpluses in the economy are generally adjusted by the forces of demand and supply. Thus it operates automatically through the price mechanism.

- ✓ **Non-interference of the State:** The State has a minimum role to play. There is no conflict between the individual interest and the society. The economic institutions function automatically preventing the interference of the government.

- ✓ **Low Cost and Qualitative Products:** The consumers and producers have full freedom and therefore it leads to production of quality products at low costs and prices.

- ✓ **Technological Improvement:** The element of competition under capitalism drives the producers to innovate something new to boost the sales and thereby bring about progress.

4.1.2.2 Disadvantages of Capitalist Economy

- ✓ **Inequalities:** Capitalism creates extreme inequalities in income and wealth. The producers, landlords, traders reap huge profits and accumulate wealth. Thus the rich become richer and the poor poorer. The poor with limited means are unable to compete with the rich. Thus capitalism widens the gap between the rich and the poor creating inequality.

- ✓ **Leads to Monopoly:** Inequality leads to monopoly. Mega corporate units replace smaller units of production. Firms combine to form cartels, trusts and in this process bring about reduction in number of firms engaged in production. They ultimately emerge as multinational corporations (MNCs) or transnational corporations (TNCs). They often hike prices against the welfare of consumer.

✓ **Depression:** There is over-production of goods due to heavy competition. The rich exploit the poor. The poor are not able to take advantage of the production and hence are exploited. At another level, over-production leads to glut in the market and hence depression. This leads to economic instabilities.

✓ **Mechanization and Automation:** Capitalism encourages mechanization and automation. This will result in unemployment particularly in labor surplus economies.

✓ **Welfare ignored:** Under capitalism, private enterprises produce luxury goods which give higher profits and ignore the basic goods required which gives less profit. Thus the welfare of public is ignored.

✓ **Exploitation of Labor:** Stringent labor laws are enacted for the exclusive profit-motive of capitalists. Fire and hire policy will become the order of the day. Such laws also help to exploit the labor by keeping their wage rate at its lowest minimum.

✓ **Basic social needs are ignored:** There are many basic social sectors like literacy, public health, poverty, drinking water, social welfare, and social security. As the profit margin in these sectors is low, capitalists will not invest. Hence most of these vital human issues will be ignored in a capitalist system.

4.1.3 Socialist Economy

In a socialist economy, the means of production are owned and operated by the State. All decisions regarding production and distribution are taken by the central planning authority. Hence the socialist economy is also called as planned economy or command economy. The government plays an active role. Social welfare is given importance; hence equal opportunity is given to all. All such advantages have delivered high level of human development. Some of the most successful socialist economies are China, Cuba, Vietnam and North Korea. The following are the basic characteristic features of socialism.

- ✓ **Social Welfare Motive:** In socialist economies, social or collective welfare will be the prime motive. Unlike capitalism, profit will not be the aim of policy making. The decisions will be taken keeping the maximum welfare of the people in mind. Thus social well-being of people will be the purpose of development.

- ✓ **Limited Right to Private Property:** The right to private property is limited. All properties of the country will be owned by the State. That is, the ownership is collective in nature. Hence no individual can accumulate too much property as in the case of capitalism.

- ✓ **Central Planning:** Most of the economic policy decisions will be taken by a centralized planning authority. Each and every sector of the economy will be directed by well designed planning.

- ✓ **No Market Forces:** In a centralized planned system of development, market forces have only a limited role to play. Production, commodity and factor prices, consumption and distribution will be governed by development planning with welfare motive.

4.1.3.1 Merits of Socialist Economy

- ✓ **Efficient use of resources:** The resources are utilized efficiently to produce socially useful goods without taking the profit margin into account. Production is increased by avoiding wastes of competition.

- ✓ **Economic Stability:** Economy is free from business fluctuations. Government plans well and everything is well coordinated to avoid over-production or unemployment. There is stability because the production and consumption of goods and services are well regulated.

- ✓ **Maximization of Social Welfare:** All citizens work for the welfare of the State. Everybody receives his or her remuneration. The State concentrates on the production of basic necessaries instead of luxury goods. The State provides free education, cheap and congenial housing, public health amenities and social security for the people.

- ✓ **Absence of Monopoly:** The elements of corporation and monopoly are eliminated since there is absence of private ownership. The state is a monopoly but produces quality goods at reasonable price.

✓ **Basic needs are met:** In socialist economies, basic human needs like water, education, health, social security, etc, are provided. Human development is more in socialist countries.

✓ **No extreme inequality:** As social welfare is the ultimate goal, there is any concentration of wealth. Extreme inequality is prevented in socialist system.

4.1.3.2 Demerits of Socialism

✓ **Bureaucratic Expansion:** A socialist economy is operated under a centralized command and control system. People here work out of fear of higher authorities. It does not give any initiative for the people to work hard.

✓ **No Freedom:** There is any freedom of occupation. Allocation of factors of production is not done rationally. Jobs are provided by the State. Place of work is also provided by the State. The consumer's choice is very limited.

✓ **Absence of Technology:** Work is monotonous and no freedom is given. Any change in the production process will alter the entire plan. Hence any innovation cannot be easily enforced. Everything is rigid and technological changes are limited.

✓ **Inefficient:** Absence of competition makes the system inefficient.

4.1.4 Mixed Economy

In a mixed economy, both public and private institutions exercise economic control. The public sector functions as a socialistic economy and the private sector as a free enterprise economy. All decisions regarding what, how and for whom to produce are taken by the State. The private sector produces and distributes goods and services. It manufactures consumer and capital goods in the interest of public welfare. A mixed economy possesses the freedom to hold private property, to earn profit, to consume, produce and distribute and to have any occupation. But if these freedoms affect public welfare adversely, they are regulated and controlled by the State. The main features of mixed economic system are:

- ✓ **Co-existence of Public and Private Sectors:** In a mixed economy, both the public and the private sectors initiatives will be there. The most strategically and nationally important sectors of the economy will be reserved for the public sector. The rest will be left for private operation. While the public sector will have social welfare as the prime motive, the private sector will function with profit motive.

- ✓ **Consolidation of merits of Capitalism and Socialism:** As seen above, both capitalism and socialism have merits and demerits. Mixed economy is expected to retain only the merits of the two systems. For instance, the government is expected to allow private investment, but the government also controls monopolies.

✓ **Planning:** Economic planning is another important feature of the mixed economy. Planning will direct the relative roles of public and private sectors and their respective jurisdictions.

4.1.4.1 Merits of Mixed Economy

✓ **Efficient resource utilization:** The resources are utilized efficiently as good features of both capitalism and socialism coexist. If there is misallocation of resources, the State controls and regulates it. This ensures the efficient utilization of resources.

✓ **Prices are administered:** The prices are not fixed always by forces of demand and supply. In the case of goods which are scarce, the prices are administered by the government and such goods are also rationed.

✓ **Social Welfare:** In a mixed economy, planning is centralized and there is overall welfare. Workers are given incentives and reward for any innovations. There is social security provided to the workers. Inequalities of income and wealth are reduced.

4.1.4.2 Demerits of Mixed Economy

✓ **Lack of Co-ordination:** The coordination between the public and private sectors is poor in a mixed economy. Public sector spends huge public resources for infrastructure. The private sector aims at profit maximization by using the infrastructure created by the public sector. But they lack social responsibility and fail to spend for public causes like health, education. The private sector also dislikes any restriction imposed on it by the government.

✓ **Red –tapism and delay by Public Sector:** There is every chance that the public sector works inefficiently. There is too much of red-tapism and corruption leading to delays in decision-making and project implementation. They result in inefficiency and also affect production.

✓ **Economic Fluctuations:** The mixed economies experience economic fluctuations. On the one hand, the private sector does not operate under very rigid conditions prescribed by the government. On the other hand, the public sector too does not operate under very rigid conditions enforced by the planned economy. The lack of policy coordination between private and public sector results in economic fluctuations.

Review of Questions

1. Write a note on traditional economy.
2. Explain the salient features of capitalism.
3. What are the merits of socialist economy?
4. What are the merits and demerits of a mixed economy?
5. What is capitalism? Explain its advantages and disadvantages.
6. Explain features, merits and demerits of socialism.
7. Explain 'mixed economy' in detail.

Chapter: 5

Economic Institutions

In modern times, economic institutions have emerged as a centre of attention in development economics after a long period. This chapter give the insight of creation, functioning and effects of Economic institutions with its definition.

5.1 Definition of Economic Institutions

- ✓ According to **Hodgson,** "Essentially, institutions are durable systems of established and embedded social rules and conventions that structure social interactions."

- ✓ According to **Schotter,** "A social institution is regularity in social behaviour that is agreed to by all members of society, specifies behaviour in specific recurrent situations, and is either self-policed or policed by some external authority."

- ✓ According to **North,** "Institutions are rules, enforcement characteristics of rules, and norms of behaviour that structure repeated human interaction."

- According to **King,** "Institutions are 'repetitive patterns of interaction through which society undertakes certain functions."

- According to **Nabli,** "Wide sense: persistent groups of norms of behaviour which serve collectively valued purposes; or in narrow sense of, a set of rules to facilitate co-ordination via allowing expectations to form."

5.2 Creation of Economic Institutions

Economic Institutions may be established by the government or it might be an initiative from private enterprise or civil society. In both cases, economic institutions are created and evolve in response to the uncertainty, risk and information costs associated with living and transacting in an imperfect world. Economic Institutions are thus rational mechanisms designed to cope with the imperfections of markets, including the asymmetry of information held by different actors, the problems that principals have in ensuring that their agents pursue the same goals. Not all institutions require the support of governments, but some do in order to remove ambiguity and to provide legal backing for the norms in question. Institutions may be seen as public goods in their benefits which are shared by all in the economy. No matter who establish them? Many institutions will require action by governments to create and implement the norm. Most institutions are not lightly changed, even when clearly imperfect or outdated. Institutions are valued for the predictability that they bring to the system; frequent change and experimentation to established norms is thus not usually encouraged. Moreover, particular institutions can confer rights and advantages to particular groups in society who will use their power to prevent changes that undermine their advantages. There is thus the possibility of path dependency in that once certain institutions are in place, then other norms and behaviours ensue, thus reinforcing patterns of development and restricting the range of options for policy. Discussion of new institutions or changes to institutions is often intense, parties recognise the implications of creating new 'rules' for the game or of changing them and each will fight for their own interests. The political economy of institutional change is therefore important in that they may evolve to confer privileges on particular groups, whether or not the institutions are efficient and effective for society as a whole, and once in place may be difficult to change. An additional consideration is that those administrating the rules may also resist change simply owing to the thereof.

5.3 Functions of Economic Institutions

The functions of economic institutions are as follows:

- ✓ The first function of economic institutions is to establish and protect property rights;
- ✓ The second function of economic institutions is to facilitate transactions;
- ✓ The third function of economic institutions is to permit economic co-operation and organisation.

5.4 Effects of Economic Institutions

The working of economic institutions largely affects three factors that help determine economic growth and development of a country. They are investment, technological innovation and economies of scale. They are as follows:

5.4.1 Effects on Investment:

This is first affect of economic institution on the working of an economy that is on investment. After establishing of a sufficient number of economic institutions, property rights become secure, it is easy to trade, retain a reasonable share of the profit, easy to obtain credit and insure against risks. With this, investment is again encouraged to increase and this leads to new capital formation.

5.4.2 Effects on Technological Innovation

Technical innovation again, secure intellectual property rights are likely to promote private investment in research and development of innovations. This is the second effects of economic institutions.

5.4.3 Effects on Economies of Scale

Economic organisation is likely to be more effective and efficient, delivering the benefits of specialisation and economies of scale where they apply, when institutions facilitate transactions and co-operation between individuals, whether in formal companies or less formal co-operatives. It is easy to imagine that there will be reinforcing interactions between the factors.

Review of Questions

1. What is Economic Institutions?
2. How Economic Institutions are created?
3. Explain different effects of Economic Institutions.

Chapter: 6

National Income Accounting

6.1 National Income

National Income is the value of aggregate output produced by different sectors during a given time periods. In real terms, it is the flow of goods and services produced in an economy in a year.

6.2 Concepts Associated with National Income

6.2.1 Gross National Product (GNP)

It is the market value of all final goods and services. These are produced by domestically owned factors of production in a country in that year.

6.2.2 Net National Product (NNP)

NNP at market price = GNP minus depreciation of capital stock.

The productive power of physical capital stock diminishes gradually because of the wear and tear that it undergoes in the process of production.

6.2.3 NNP at factor cost or National Income

NNP at factor cost = NNP at market price minus Indirect Business Tax minus Non tax liabilities minus Business Transfer Payments plus Subsidy from Government = National Income.

6.2.4 Gross Domestic Product (GDP)

GDP is the sum total of values of all goods and services produced within the geographical boundary of the country; these are without adding the factor income received from abroad.

6.3 Distinction between Gross National Product and Gross Domestic Product –

Gross National Product (GNP) is different from Gross Domestic Product (GDP) in following respects: Firstly, GNP refers to the total market value of all the final goods and services produced in a country during a given year, plus net factor income from abroad. But GDP refers to the total market value of all the goods and services produced in the given year within the domestic territory of the country. Secondly, GNP includes all income earned by the country in abroad (including foreign investments). But GDP does not include the income earned by the country from abroad.

6.4 Methods of measurement of National Income

There are three alternative ways of estimating National Income of a country. Broadly it may be viewed from income side, output side and expenditure side. Let us discuss these methods:

6.4.1 Product method

Product method implies by adding the values of output produced and services rendered by different sectors. This method is unscientific. Only those goods and services are counted which are paid for, that is marketed. The value added method can be used. Here only the value added by each firm in the production process is included in the output figure. The value added output of all sectors makes up GNP at factor cost.

6.4.2 Income method

All income from employment and ownership of assets before taxation received from productive activities to be counted in Income method. The undistributed profits of the private sector are added into it. The trading surplus of the public sector corporations is also added in this. These exclude some items which do not arise from productive activities, such as — sickness benefits, interest on national debt etc.

6.4.3 Expenditure Method

This method depends on by measuring the total domestic expenditure. It comprises two elements and they are consumption expenditure of the household sector on goods and services and consumption outlays of business sector and public authorities. In this method, investment expenditure is used for making a fixed capital like building, machinery etc.

6.5 Usefulness of National Income estimates

✓ It shows how the production is changing, to output and the effects of government policies and programmes.

- ✓ In analyzing the relation between input of one industry and the output of the other.
- ✓ It reveals the distribution of income among economic units.
- ✓ Changes of tastes and fashions are revealed which help businessmen in deciding what to produce or for whom to produce.
- ✓ The national income quantum indicates the ability of a country to pay its share for international purpose e.g. membership of IMF or World Bank.

6.6 Difficulties in Estimating National Income

- ✓ No practicable methods exists for inclusion of some items in National Income (NI), such as — services for which no remuneration is paid, goods that are marketed sold at a price but are used for self-consumption etc.
- ✓ It is not always possible to make a clear distinction between primary, intermediate and final goods.
- ✓ The price that should be chosen to determine the money value of National product is a difficult question.
- ✓ Debate regarding inclusion of income of foreign companies in National Income estimates since, a large part of such income is remitted out of the country.
- ✓ Changes in the price level involve the use of Index Numbers which have their inherent difficulties.
- ✓ Official statistics are not always accurate as it is based on guess work and sample survey.

✓ Methods of computing NI are not the same in all countries. •
The statistical data are often not available.

Review of Questions

1. What is National Income?

2. Explain the different concepts associated to the National Income.

3. Describe the methods of measurement of National Income.

Chapter: 7

Saving and Investment

7.1 Savings and Investment

Saving and investment are the basic economic activities of an economy. Saving is inevitable for capital formation and economic growth. Saving itself has nothing to do with economic growth unless savings are properly mobilized and effectively channelized and invested to enhance capital stock to increase production and wealth of the economy. Thus aggregate savings and investment are equal.

But they may not be always in equilibrium. The classical economists believed that savings were automatically invested. They thought the decisions to save and the decisions to invest were made by the same persons. But Keynes argued that saving and investment were made by different persons for different reasons and were influenced by different factors. Thus, sometimes savings might exceed investment. When this happened, there would be deficiency of aggregate demand and general unemployment. Keynes thought the gap between S and I could be filled by government intervention either directly by increasing government expenditure or indirectly by actions influencing the supply of money

Thus $S = I$ .... (1)

Therefore $Y = C + I$ .... (2)

Or $Y = C + S$ .... (3)

7.2 Saving Function

The portion of the income not spent on consumption is saving. Saving is consumption forgone. If saving rises, consumption will fall. According to Keynes, the level of saving in the economy, like consumption, depends basically on income. The relationship between saving and income can mathematically be expressed as in equation (5) and that is called as saving function.

$S = -a + by$ .... (4)

$S = -4 + .2Y$ .... (5)

Where S – Saving;

Y = Income;

-a = dis-savings.

Marginal Propensity to Save (MPS) is the ratio of change in saving to a change in income. Thus it is the rate of change in the propensity to save.

Or $MPC = \dfrac{\Delta S}{\Delta Y}$ .... (6)

Where ΔS - Change in saving and ΔY - Change in income

With an increase income, if MPC tends to fall, MPS will tend to rise. If MPC remains constant, MPS also will remain constant. Thus income consists of consumption and saving.

Hence $Y = C + S$ .... (7)

Or $MPC + MPS = 1$ .... (8)

$MPS = 1 - MPC$ or .... (9)

$MPC = 1 - MPS$ .... (10)

In an economy where people spend less of their additional income, MPC will be less and the CC curve will be less steep. Note that the constant (-a) is dis-saving because it is autonomous consumption which is unrelated to income. The autonomous consumption will became zero in the long run. That is, households cannot consume without income in the long run. Hence in the long run, the consumption purely depends upon income and the curve C starts from origin.

7.3 Investment Function

Investment has a specific meaning in economics. It means additions to the existing productive capacities (stock of fixed capital and inventories). They include fixed equipments, machinery, building, raw materials, replacement due to depreciation, etc. It lays down the basis for future production. Investment is the key structural component of total spending or aggregate spending. By investment, Keynes means real investment and not financial investment. Investment is the addition to real capital assets. It does not mean the purchase of bonds or shares which are financial investment. The distinction between consumption and investment is fundamental in

Keynesian theory. Importance of investment as a component of aggregate demand rises due to the fact that it is another major component. Consumption is a stable function of income. So it was not possible to change aggregate demand by changing consumption expenditure as it depends on income. Keynes found that investment is an autonomous expenditure determined independently of the level of income. He found it to be the major cause for the variation and instability in income and employment. The worldwide depression of 1930s was also caused by a fall in investment.

7.4 Determinants of Investment

According to Keynes, employment depends on investment. Employment fluctuates on account of fluctuations in investment. Therefore, we must discuss what determines the amount of investment. Investment spending is determined by Expectations of future profitability or business confidence and Rate of interest. Firms invest either from their own profits or by borrowing. Households having saving, have to decide whether to invest the money for profit or lend/deposit for interest. If the expected profit is higher than the rate of interest, then the households will invest. Otherwise they will lend or deposit their money for interest. Firms who invest their own profit will also decide in the same manner. Suppose the firms borrow for investment, then they have to pay interest for that. Hence, firms will invest borrowed money only when the expected profit is high enough to pay the interest and the cost of initial capital. Thus, in all the above cases, the decision to invest will be based on the rate of interest and business confidence. Of these two, business confidence or expectations about future profitability has got greater significance than the rate of interest. This is because rate of interest is stable in the short run. The expectations about profitability involve several considerations of the future about which there cannot be any certainty. Bleak prospects will lead to a reduction of investment and it will affect employment and vice versa.

Review of Questions

1. What is saving?
2. Define Investment?
3. Explain the saving and investment functions.

Chapter: 8

Demand and Supply

Demand and Supply is one of the most basic concepts of economics and it is the backbone of any economy. Demand refers to how much quantity of a product or service is desired by buyers. The term demand is used in economics in a special sense. Generally, we use the term desire, want and demand to convey the same meaning. But in economics, all the terms have separate meanings. Desire is just a wishful thinking. It will not be called demand. Likewise, if you have enough money but you are not willing to spend, then this desire will be called want but not demand. The quantity demanded is the amount of a product people are willing to buy at a certain price; the relationship between price and quantity demanded is known as the demand relationship. Supply represents how much the market can offer. The quantity supplied refers to the amount of a certain good producers are willing to supply when receiving a certain price. The correlation between price and how much of a good or service is supplied to the market is known as the supply relationship.

8.1 The Law of Demand

The law of demand states that, if all other factors remain equal, the higher the price of a good, the less people will demand that good. In other words, if other things being equal, the demand for a good extends with a fall in price and contracts with a rise in price. The amount of a good that buyers purchase at a higher price is less because as the price of a good goes up, so does the opportunity cost of buying that good. As a result, people will naturally avoid buying a product that will force them to shift the consumption of something else they value more. The graph below shows that the curve is a downward slope.

Figure1: Demand Curve

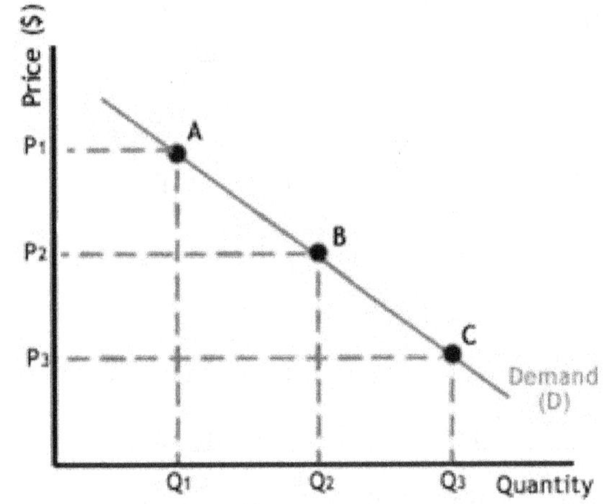

A, B and C are points on the demand curve. Each point on the curve reflects a direct correlation between quantities demanded (Q) and price (P). So, at point A, the quantity demanded will be Q1 and the

64

price will be P1, and so on. The demand relationship curve illustrates the negative relationship between price and quantity demanded. The higher the price of a good the lower the quantity demanded (A), and the lower the price, the more the good will be in demand (C).

8.2 The Law of Supply

Like the law of demand, the law of supply demonstrates the quantities that will be sold at a certain price. But unlike the law of demand, the supply relationship shows an upward slope. This means that the higher the price, the higher the quantity supplied. Producers supply more at a higher price because selling a higher quantity at a higher price increases revenue. A, B and C are points on the supply curve. Each point on the curve reflects a direct correlation between quantity supplied (Q) and price (P). At point B, the quantity supplied will be Q2 and the price will be P2, and so on.

Figure 2: Supply Curve

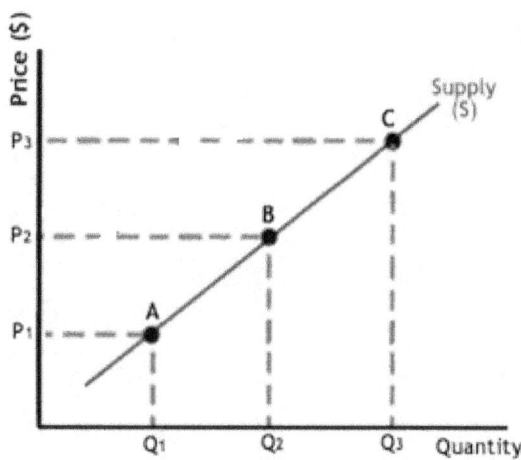

8.3 Supply and Demand Relationship

Now that we know the laws of supply and demand, let's turn to an example to show how supply and demand affect price. Imagine that a special edition CD of your favorite band is released for $20. Because the record company's previous analysis showed that consumers will not demand CDs at a price higher than $20, only ten CDs were released because the opportunity cost is too high for suppliers to produce more. If, however, the ten CDs are demanded by 20 people, the price will subsequently rise because, according to the demand relationship, as demand increases, so does the price. Consequently, the rise in price should prompt more CDs to be supplied as the supply relationship shows that the higher the price, the higher the quantity supplied. If, however, there are 30 CDs produced and demand is still at 20, the price will not be pushed up because the supply more than accommodates demand. In fact after the 20 consumers have been satisfied with their CD purchases, the price of the leftover CDs may drop as CD producers attempt to sell the remaining ten CDs. The lower price will then make the CD more available to people who had previously decided that the opportunity cost of buying the CD at $20 was too high.

8.4 Equilibrium

When supply and demand are equal (i.e. when the supply function and demand function intersect) the economy is said to be at equilibrium. At this point, the allocation of goods is at its most efficient because the amount of goods being supplied is exactly the same as the amount of goods being demanded. Thus, everyone (individuals, firms, or countries) is satisfied with the current economic condition. At the given price, suppliers are selling all the goods that they have produced and consumers are getting all the goods that they are demanding. As you can see on the chart, equilibrium occurs at the intersection of the demand and supply curve, which indicates no allocation inefficiency. At this point, the price of the goods will be P* and the quantity will be Q*. These figures are referred to as equilibrium price and quantity. In the real market place equilibrium can only ever be reached in theory, so the prices of goods and services are constantly changing in relation to fluctuations in demand and supply.

Figure 3: Equilibrium position

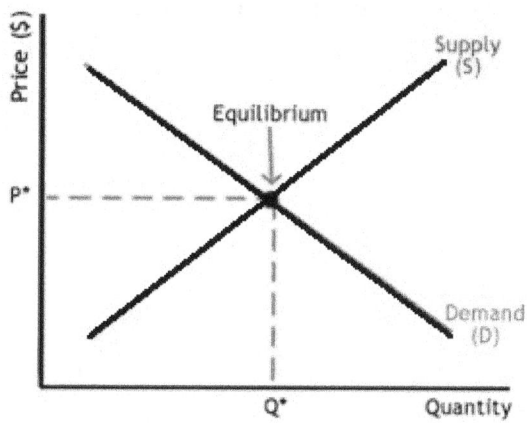

8.5 Disequilibrium

Disequilibrium occurs whenever the price or quantity is not equal to P* or Q*.

8.5.1 Excess Supply

If the price is set too high, excess supply will be created within the economy and there will be allocate inefficiency.

67

Figure 4: Excess Supply Curve

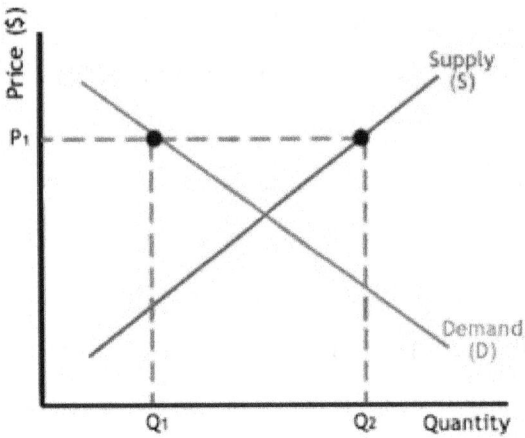

8.5.2 Excess Demand

Excess demand is created when price is set below the equilibrium price. Because the price is so low, too many consumers

Figure 5: Excess Demand Curve

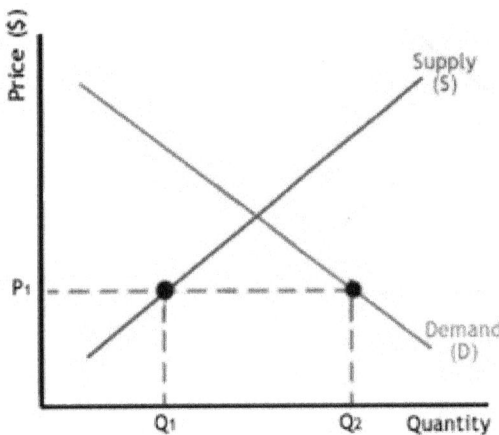

want the good while producers are not making enough of it. In this situation, at price P1, the quantity of goods demanded by consumers at this price is Q2. Conversely, the quantity of goods that producers are willing to produce at this price is Q1. Thus, there are too few goods being produced to satisfy the wants (demand) of the consumers. However, as consumers have to compete with one other to buy the good at this price, the demand will push the price up, making suppliers want to supply more and bringing the price closer to its equilibrium.

8.6 Shifts vs. Movement

For economics, the "movements" and "shifts" in relation to the supply and demand curves represent very different market phenomena:

8.6.1 Movements

A movement refers to a change along a curve. On the demand curve, a movement denotes a change in both price and quantity demanded from one point to another on the curve. The movement implies that the demand relationship remains consistent. Therefore, a movement along the demand curve will occur when the price of the good changes and the quantity demanded changes in accordance to the original demand relationship. In other words, a movement occurs when a change in the quantity demanded is caused only by a change in price, and vice versa. Like a movement along the demand curve, a movement along the supply curve means that the supply relationship remains consistent. Therefore, a movement along the supply curve will occur when the price of the good changes and the quantity supplied changes in accordance to the original supply relationship. In other words, a movement occurs when a change in quantity supplied is caused only by a change in price, and vice versa.

Figure 6:

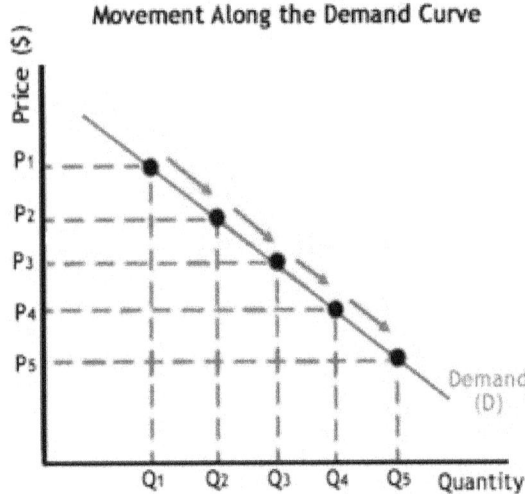

Figure 7:

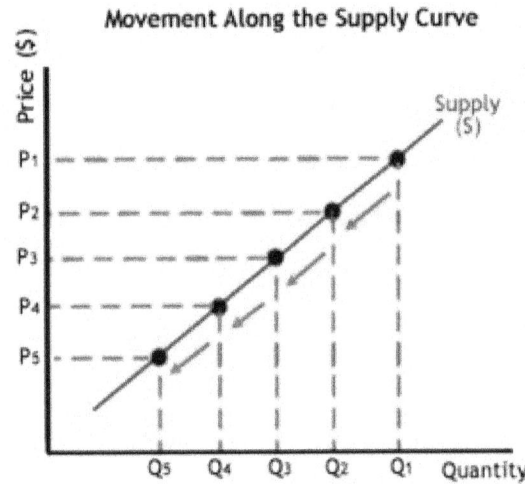

8.6.2 Shifts

A shift in a demand or supply curve occurs when a good's quantity demanded or supplied changes even though price remains the same. For instance, if the price for a bottle of beer was $2 and the quantity of beer demanded increased from Q1 to Q2, then there would be a shift in the demand for beer. Shifts in the demand curve imply that the original demand relationship has changed, meaning that quantity demand is affected by a factor other than price. A shift in the demand relationship would occur if, for instance, beer suddenly became the only type of alcohol available for consumption.

Figure 8:

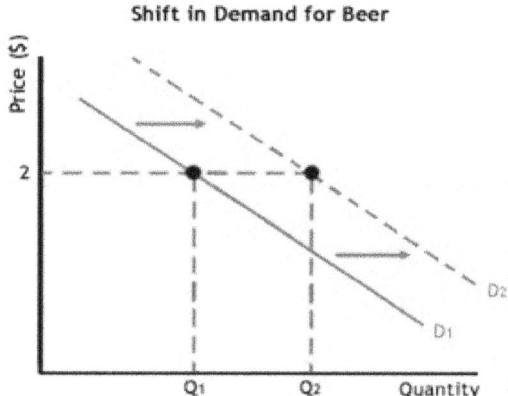

Figure 9:

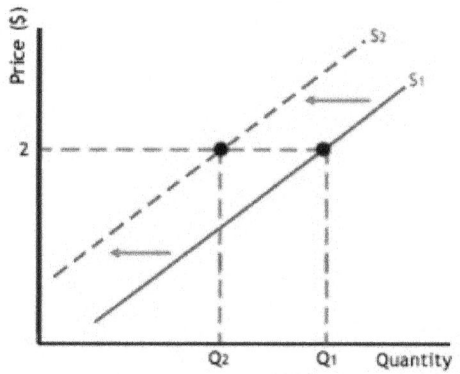

Conversely, if the price for a bottle of beer was $2 and the quantity supplied decreased from Q1 to Q2, then there would be a shift in the supply of beer. Like a shift in the demand curve, a shift in the supply curve implies that the original supply curve has changed, meaning that the quantity supplied is affected by a factor other than price. A shift in the supply curve would occur if, for instance, a natural disaster caused a mass shortage of hops; beer manufacturers would be forced to supply less beer for the same price.

Review of Questions
1. What is Law of Demand?
2. Define Law of Supply?
3. Define Equilibrium.
4. Explain shift and movement of Demand and supply.

Chapter: 9

Elasticity

9.1 Elasticity

Since the laws of supply and demand set price, prices are always subject to change based upon market forces and the interaction between the consumer and business. This change in prices and the degree of said change is known as *elasticity*.

There are two types of elasticity that we need to be concerned with. They are demand elasticity and supply elasticity.

9.2 Demand Elasticity

Demand elasticity is the degree to which changes in price effect changes in demand. Demand is elastic when a small change in price effects a large change in demand. Such products that show great variability in demand are known to have elastic demand. Demand is inelastic when a change in price does not bring about a correspondingly large change in demand, or any change at all. Said products are known to show inelastic demand. How can we tell if an item is will be elastic or inelastic? The elasticity of demand can usually be estimated by examining the answers to three key questions. All three answers do not have to be the same in order to determine elasticity, and in some cases the answer to a single question is so important that it alone might dominate the answers of the other two. Let's examine the three questions.

9.3 Elasticity of Supply

When supply goes up price goes down and when price goes up supply goes down. Products are elastic if price has a large impact on supply; they are inelastic if supply remains relatively constant due to fluctuations in price. Factors which effect supply elasticity are: Price, resource costs, technology, competitive products, profit expectations, number of sellers, natural events, taxes, subsidies and government regulations, overproduction, flooding the market, inability to produce an item, scarcity of natural resources. The degree to which a demand or supply curve reacts to a change in price is the curve's elasticity. Elasticity varies among products because some products may be more essential to the consumer. Products that are necessities are more insensitive to price changes because consumers would continue buying these products despite price increases. Conversely, a price increase of a good or service that is considered less of a necessity will deter more consumers because the

74

opportunity ost of buying the product will become too high. A good or service is considered to be highly elastic if a slight change in price leads to a sharp change in the quantity demanded or supplied. Usually these kinds of products are readily available in the market and a person may not necessarily need them in his or her daily life. On the other hand, an inelastic good or service is one in which changes in price witness only modest changes in the quantity demanded or supplied, if any at all. These goods tend to be things that are more of a necessity to the consumer in his or her daily life. To determine the elasticity of the supply or demand curves, we can use this simple equation:

Elasticity = (% change in quantity / % change in price) ... (1)

If elasticity is greater than or equal to one, the curve is considered to be elastic. If it is less than one, the curve is said to be inelastic. As we mentioned previously, the demand curve is a negative slope, and if there is a large decrease in the quantity demanded with a small increase in price, the demand curve looks flatter, or more horizontal. This flatter curve means that the good or service in question is elastic. Meanwhile, inelastic demand is represented with a much more upright curve as quantity changes little with a large movement in price. Elasticity of supply works similarly. If a change in price results in a big change in the amount supplied, the supply curve appears flatter and is considered elastic. Elasticity in this case would be greater than or equal to one. On the other hand, if a big change in price only results in a minor change in the quantity supplied, the supply curve is steeper and its elasticity would be less than one.

Figure 1: Elastic Demand

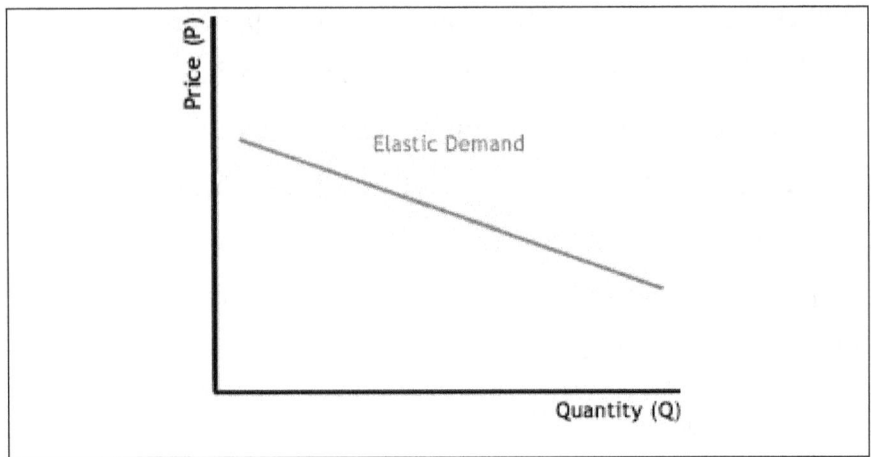

Figure 2: Inelastic Demand

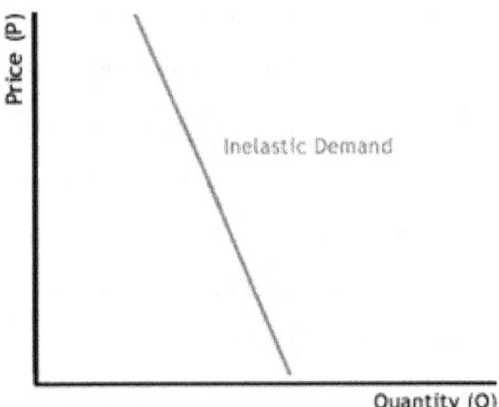

Figure 3: Elastic Supply

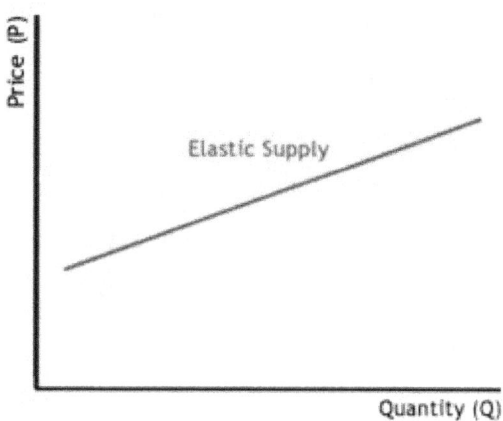

Figure 4: Inelastic Supply

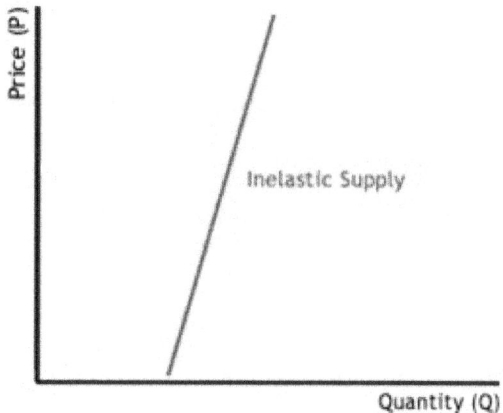

9.3 Factors Affecting Demand Elasticity

There are three main factors that influence a demand's price elasticity:

✓ **The availability of substitutes -** This is probably the most important factor influencing the elasticity of a good or service. In general, the more substitutes, the more elastic the demand will be.

- ✓ **Amount of income available to spend on the good -** This factor affecting demand elasticity refers to the total a person can spend on a particular good or service. Thus if there is an increase in price and no change in the amount of income available to spend on the good, there will be an elastic reaction in demand; demand will be sensitive to a change in price if there is no change in income.
- ✓ **Time -** The third influential factor is time.

9.4 Price elasticity of demand

Price elasticity of demand (PED or E_d) is a measure used in economics to show the responsiveness of the quantity demanded of a good or service to a change in its price, if others things remain. More precisely, it gives the percentage change in quantity demanded in response to a one percent change in price. Price elasticity is almost always negative, although analysts tend to ignore the sign even though this can lead to ambiguity. Only goods which do not conform to the law of demand, such as Veblen and Giffen goods, have a positive Price elasticity of demand. In general, the demand for a good is said to be inelastic when the Price elasticity of demand is less than one (in absolute value): that is, changes in price have a relatively small effect on the quantity of the good demanded. The demand for a good is said to be elastic when its Price elasticity of demand is greater than one that is, changes in price have a relatively large effect on the quantity of a good demanded.

9.4 Income Elasticity of Demand

In the second factor outlined above, we saw that if price increases while income stays the same, demand will decrease. It follows, then, that if there is an increase in income, demand tends to increase as well. The degree to which an increase in income will cause an increase in demand is called income elasticity of demand, With some goods and services, we may actually notice a decrease in demand as income increases. These are considered goods and services of inferior quality that will be dropped by a consumer who receives a salary increase. An example may be the increase in the demand of DVDs as opposed to video cassettes, which are generally considered to be of lower quality. Products for which the demand decreases as income increases have an income elasticity of less than zero. Products that witness no change in demand despite a change in income usually have an income elasticity of zero - these goods and services are considered necessities.

9.6 Cross elasticity of demand

In economics, the cross elasticity of demand or cross-price elasticity of demand measures the responsiveness of the quantity demanded for a good to a change in the price of another good, ceteris paribus. It is measured as the percentage change in quantity demanded for the first good that occurs in response to a percentage change in price of the second good. A negative cross elasticity denotes two products that are complements, while a positive cross elasticity denotes two substitute products. Assume products A and B are *complements*, meaning that an increase in the demand for A accompanies an increase in the quantity demanded for B. Therefore, if the price of product B decreases, the demand curve for product A shifts to the right, increasing A's demand, resulting in a *negative* value for the cross elasticity of demand. The exact opposite reasoning holds for substitutes.

In the case of perfect substitutes, the cross elasticity of demand is equal to positive infinity (at the point when both goods can be consumed). Where the two goods are *independent*, or, as described in consumer theory, if a good is independent in demand then the demand of that good is independent of the quantity consumed of all other goods available to the consumer, the cross elasticity of demand will be *zero* i.e. if the price of one good changes, there will be no change in demand for the other good. When goods are substitutable, the diversion ratio, which quantifies how much of the displaced demand for product j switches to product i, is measured by the ratio of the cross-elasticity to the own-elasticity multiplied by the ratio of product i's demand to product j's demand. In the discrete case, the diversion ratio is naturally interpreted as the fraction of product j demand which treats product i as a second choice, measuring how much of the demand diverting from product j because of a price increase is diverted to product i can be written as the product of the ratio of the cross-elasticity to the own-elasticity and the ratio of the demand for product i to the demand for product j. In some cases, it has a natural interpretation as the proportion of people buying product j who would consider product i their "second choice".

Review of Questions

1. What is Elasticity of Demand?
2. Define Price Elasticity of Demand?
3. Define Income Elasticity of Demand.
4. Explain the factors affecting of elasticity of Demand.

Chapter: 10

Utility

10.1 Concept of Utility

In the ordinary language, 'utility' means 'usefulness'. In Economics, utility is defined as the power of a commodity or a service to satisfy a human want. Utility is a subjective or psychological concept. The same commodity or service gives different utilities to different people. For a vegetarian, mutton has no utility. Warm clothes have little utility for the people in hot countries. So utility depends on the consumer and his need for the commodity.

10.2 Total Utility

Total Utility refers to the sum of utilities of all units of a commodity consumed. For example, if a consumer consumes ten biscuits, then the total utility is the sum of satisfaction of consuming all the ten biscuits.

10.3 Marginal Utility

Marginal Utility is the addition made to the total utility by consuming one more unit of a commodity. For example, if a consumer consumes 10 biscuits, the marginal utility is the utility derived from the 10th unit. It is nothing but the total utility of 10 biscuits minus the total utility of 9 biscuits.

Thus $MU_n = TU_n - TU_{n-1}$ ... (1)

Where MU_n = Marginal Utility of 'nth' commodity.

TU_n = Total Utility of n units.

TU_{n-1} = Total Utility of n-1 units.

Table 10.1: Relationship between Marginal Utility and Total Utility

Sr. No.	Marginal Utility	Total Utility
1	Declines	Increase
2	zero	Reaches Maximum
3	Negative	Declines

10.4 Law of Diminishing Marginal Utility

The law of diminishing marginal utility explains an ordinary experience of a consumer. If a consumer takes more and more units of a commodity, the additional utility he derives from an extra unit of the commodity goes on falling. Thus, according to this law, the marginal utility decreases with the increase in the consumption of a commodity. When marginal utility decreases, the total utility increases at a diminishing rate. Gossen, Bentham, Jevons, Karl Menger contributed initially for the development of these ideas. But Alfred Marshall perfected these ideas and made it as a law. This Law is also known as Gossen's I Law.

10.4.1 Definition

According to Marshall, "*The additional benefit which a person derives from a given increase of his stock of a thing diminishes with every increase in the stock that he already has*".

10.4.2 Assumptions of the Law

- ✓ The units of consumption must be in standard units e.g., a cup of tea, a bottle of cool drink etc.
- ✓ All the units of the commodity must be identical in all aspects like taste, quality, color and size.
- ✓ The law holds good only when the process of consumption continues without any time gap.
- ✓ The consumer's taste, habit or preference must remain the same during the process of consumption.
- ✓ The income of the consumer remains constant.
- ✓ The prices of the commodity consumed and its substitutes are constant.
- ✓ The consumer is assumed to be a rational economic man. As a rational consumer, he wants to maximize the total utility.
- ✓ Utility is measurable.

10.4.3 Explanation

Suppose Mr X is hungry and eats apple one by one. The first apple gives him great pleasure (higher utility) as he is hungry; when he takes the second apple, the extent of his hunger will reduce. Therefore he will derive less utility from the second apple. If he continues to take additional apples, the utility derived from the third apple will be less than that of the second one. In this way, the additional utility (marginal utility) from the extra units will go on decreasing. If the consumer continues to take more apples, marginal utility falls to zero and then becomes negative.

Tables 10.2:

Units of Apple	Total utility	Marginal Utility
1	20	20
2	35	15
3	45	10
4	50	5
5	50	0
6	45	-5
7	35	-10

Table 2 gives the utility derived by a person from successive units of consumption of apples. From above table, it is very clear that the marginal utility (addition made to the total utility) goes on declining. The consumer derives 20 units of utility from the first apple he consumes. When he consumes the apples continuously, the marginal utility falls to 5 units for the fourth apple and becomes zero for the fifth apple. The marginal utilities are negative for the 6th and 7th apples. Thus when the consumer consumes a commodity continuously, the marginal utility declines, reaches zero and then becomes negative. The total utility (sum of utilities of all the units consumed) goes on increasing and after a certain stage begins to decline. When the marginal utility declines and it is greater than zero, the total utility increases. For the first four units of apple, the total utility increases from 20 units to 50 units. When the marginal utility is zero (5th apple), the total utility is constant (50 units) and reaches the maximum. When the marginal utility becomes negative (6th and 7th units), the total utility declines from 50 units to 45 and then to 35 units.

10.4.4 Importance of Law of Diminishing Marginal Utility

- ✓ The Law of Diminishing Marginal Utility is the foundation for various other economic laws. For example, the Law of Demand is the result of the operation of the Law of Diminishing Marginal Utility. In other words, as more and more units of a commodity are consumed, each of them gives less and less marginal utility. This is due to the operation of the Law of DMU. As utility falls, consumer is therefore willing to pay a lower price only.

- ✓ The Law of DMU operates in the case of money also. A rich man already possesses a lot of money. If more and more money is newly added to his income, marginal utility of money begins to fall. Alfred Marshall assumed that the marginal utility of money remains constant.

- ✓ This law is a handy tool for the Finance Minister for increasing tax rate on the rich.
- ✓ Producers are guided by the operation the Law of DMU, unconsciously. They constantly change the design, the package of their goods so that the goods become more attractive to the consumers and they appear as 'new goods'. Or else, the consumers would think that they are using the same commodity, over and over. In such a situation, the Law of DMU operates in the minds of the consumers. Demand for such commodities may fall.

10.4.5 Criticism

The Law of DMU is criticized on the following grounds.

- ✓ Deriving utility is a psychological experience, when we say a unit of X gives ten units of utility; this means that utility can be measured precisely. In reality, utility cannot be measured. For example, when a person sees a film and says it is very good, we cannot measure the utility he has derived from it. However, we can measure utility indirectly by the cinema fare he is willing to pay.
- ✓ The Law is based on a single commodity consumption mode. That is, a consumer consumes only one good at a time. This is an unrealistic assumption. In real life, a consumer consumes more than one good at a time.
- ✓ According to the Law, a consumer should consume successive units of the same good continuously. In real life it is not so.

- ✓ The Law assumes constancy of the marginal utility of money. This means the marginal utility of money remains constant, even when money stock changes. In real life, the marginal utility derived from the consumption of a good cannot be measured precisely in monetary terms.
- ✓ As utility itself is capable of varying from person to person, marginal utility derived from the consumption of a good cannot be measured precisely.
- ✓

10.5 Law of Equi-Marginal Utility

The idea of equi-marginal principle was first mentioned by H.H.Gossen (1810-1858) of Germany. Hence it is called Gossen's second Law. Alfred Marshall made significant refinements of this law in his '*Principles of Economics*'. The law of equi-marginal utility explains the behavior of a consumer when he consumers more than one commodity. Wants are unlimited

but the income which is available to the consumers to satisfy all his wants is limited. This law explains how the consumer spends his limited income on various commodities to get maximum satisfaction. The law of equi-marginal utility is also known as the law of substitution or the

law of maximum satisfaction or the principle of proportionality between prices and marginal utility.

10.5.1 Definition

In the words of Prof. Marshall, "If a person has a thing which can be put to several uses, he will distribute it among these uses in such a way that it has the same marginal utility in all".

10.5.2 Assumptions

- ✓ The consumer is rational so he wants to get maximum satisfaction.
- ✓ The utility of each commodity is measurable.
- ✓ The marginal utility of money remains constant.
- ✓ The income of the consumer is given.
- ✓ The prices of the commodities are given.
- ✓ The law is based on the law of diminishing marginal utility.

10.5.3 Explanation of the law

Suppose there are two goods X and Y on which a consumer has to spend a given income. The consumer being rational, he will try to spend his limited income on goods X and Y to maximize his total utility or satisfaction. Only at that point the consumer will be in equilibrium. According to the law of equi-marginal utility, the consumer will be in equilibrium at the point where the utility derived from the last rupee spent on each is equal.

10.5.4 Limitations of the Law

The law of equi-marginal utility bristles with the following difficulties.

- ✓ **Indivisibility of Goods:** The theory is weakened by the fact that many commodities like a car, a house etc. are indivisible. In the case of indivisible goods, the law is not applicable.

- ✓ **The Marginal Utility of Money is not Constant:** The theory is based on the assumption that the marginal utility of money is constant. But that is not really so.

- ✓ **The Measurement of Utility is not possible:** Marshall states that the price a consumer is willing to pay for a commodity is equal to its marginal utility. But modern economists argue that, if two persons are paying an equal price for given commodity, it does not mean that both are getting the same level of utility. Thus utility is a subjective concept, which cannot be measured, in quantitative terms.

- ✓ **Utilities are Interdependent:** This law assumes that commodities are independent and therefore their marginal utilities are also independent. But in real life commodities are either substitutes or complements. Their utilities are therefore interdependent.

Review of Questions

1. What is Utility?
2. Define Total Utility?
3. Define Marginal Utility.
4. Explain the Law of Equi- Marginal Utility.
5. Describe the Law of Diminishing Marginal Utility.

Chapter: 11

Production

11.1 Meaning of Production

Production in Economics refers to the creation of those goods and services which have exchange value. It means the creation of utilities. These utilities are in the nature of form utility, time utility and place utility. Creation of such utilities results in the overall increase in the production and redistribution of goods and services in the economy. Utility of a commodity may increase due to several reasons.

- ✓ **Form Utility:** If the physical form of a commodity is changed, its utility may increase. For instance, the utility of cotton increases, if it is converted into clothes. The other examples are processing of paddy into rice, wheat into flour and butter into ghee.

- ✓ **Place Utility:** If a commodity is transported from one place to another, its utility may increase. For instance, if rice is transported from Tamil Nadu to Kerala, its utility will be more.

91

- ✓ **Time Utility:** If the commodity is stored for future usage, its utility may increase. During rainy season, water is stored in reservoirs and it is used at a later time. This increases the utility of that stored water. Agricultural commodities like paddy, wheat, oilseeds, pulses are stored for the regular uses of consumers throughout the year.

- ✓ **Possession Utility:** Commodities in the transaction process, change from one person to another person. Commodities in the hands of producers have some utility and by the time they reach consumers through the traders their utility is increased. Such utility due to possession or transfer of ownership of the commodity is called, possession utility. For example, paddy in the hands of producers, i.e. farmers has less utility compared to that of the rice in the hands of consumers.

11.2 Factors of production

Human activity can be broken down into two components, production and consumption. When there is production, a process of transformation takes place. Inputs are converted into an output. The inputs are classified and referred to as land, labour, and capital. Collectively the inputs are called factors of production. When the factors of production are combined in order to produce something, a fourth factor is required. Goods and services do not produce themselves but need some conscious thought process in order to plan and implement manufacture. This thought process is often called entrepreneurship or organization. Factors of production refer to those goods and services which help in the productive process.

11.3 Kinds of factors of production

Factors of production are broadly classified into primary factors and derived factors. Man (Labour) acts upon Nature (Land) to produce goods and services and wealth. These two factors (Land and Labour) are naturally given and without them no goods can be produced. These are called primary factors. Capital and organization are derived from the primary factors of production, and are called derived factors of production. These derived factors of production, when combined with the primary factors of production, raise total production. According to the traditional classification, there are four factors of production. They are Land, Labour, Capital and Organization.

11.4 Land

Land as a factor of production refers to all those natural resources or gifts of nature which are provided free to man by the nature. It includes within itself several things such as land surface, air, water, minerals, forests, rivers, lakes, seas, mountains, climate and weather. Thus, 'Land' includes all things that are not made by man but by the nature. Land is divided into the boundaries of so many countries on Earth by the man.

11.4.1 Characteristics of land

Characteristic of Land is given below:

- ✓ Land is a free gift of nature.
- ✓ Land is fixed (inelastic) in supply.
- ✓ Land is imperishable.
- ✓ Land is immobile.

- ✓ Land differs in fertility and situation.
- ✓ Land is a passive factor of production.

As a gift of nature, the initial supply price of land is zero because of only living planet that is our earth. However, when used in production, it becomes scarce. Therefore, it fetches a price, accordingly.

11.5 Labour

Labour is the human input into the production process. Alferd Marshall defines labour as 'the use or exertion of body or mind, partly or wholly, with a view to secure an income apart from the pleasure derived from the work'.

11.5.1 Characteristics or Peculiarities of labour

- ✓ Labour is perishable.
- ✓ Labour is an active factor of production. Neither land nor capital can yield much without labour.
- ✓ Labour is not homogeneous. Skill and dexterity vary from person to person.
- ✓ Labour cannot be separated from the laborer.
- ✓ Labour is mobile. Man moves from one place to another from a low paid occupation to a high paid occupation.
- ✓ Individual labour has only limited bargaining power. He cannot fight with his employer for a rise in wages or improvement in workplace conditions. However, when workers combine to form trade unions, the bargaining power of labour increases.

Labour can assume several forms. Digging earth, breaking stones, carrying loads comprise simple labour operations but labour also covers highly qualified and skilled managers, engineers and technicians.

11.5.2 Division of Labour

The concept 'Division of Labour' was introduced by Adam Smith in his book 'An Enquiry into The Nature and Causes of Wealth of Nations'.

11.5.2.1 Meaning of Division of Labour

Division of Labour means dividing the process of production into distinct and several component processes and assigning each component in the hands of a labour or a set of laborers, who are specialists in that particular process. For example, a tailor stitches a shirt in full. In the case of garment exporters, cutting of cloth, stitching of hands, body, collars, holes for buttons, stitching of buttons, etc., are done independently by different workers. Therefore, they are combining the parts into a whole shirt. A tailor may stitch a maximum of four shirts a day. In the case of garment exports firm, it may stitch more than 100 shirts a day. Thus, division of labour results in increased production.

11.5.2.2 Division of Labour and Market

It is stated "Division of Labour is limited by the extent of market". When markets for a commodity grows from local to national and national to international, producers of that commodity divide and subdivide the processes of its production into finer and finer divisions of labour. Each sub-division is assigned to a particular set of specialist workers. As a result, production rises enormously.

11.5.2.3 Merits of Division of Labour

- ✓ Division of labour improves efficiency of labour when labour repeats doing the same tasks.
- ✓ Facilitates the use of machinery in production, resulting in inventions. E.g. More's telegraphic codes.
- ✓ Time and materials are put to the best and most efficient use.

11.5.2.4 Demerits of Division of Labour

The demerits of Division of Labour are:

- ✓ Repetition of the same task makes labour to feel that the work is monotonous and stale. It kills the humanity in him.
- ✓ Narrow specialization reduces the possibility of labour to find alternative avenues of employment. This results in increased unemployment.
- ✓ Kills the growth of handicrafts and the worker loses the satisfaction of having made a commodity in full.

11.6 Capital

Capital is the man made physical goods used to produce other goods and services. In the ordinary language, capital means money. In Economics, capital refers to that part of man-made wealth which is used for the further production of wealth. According to Marshall, "Capital consists of those kinds of wealth other than free gifts of nature, which yield income". Money is regarded as capital because it can be used to buy raw materials, tools, implements and machinery for production. The terms capital and wealth are not synonymous. Capital is that part of wealth which is used for the further production of wealth. Thus, all wealth is not capital but all capital is wealth. The process through which capital is required for further increase in income is called capital formation.

11.6.1 Forms of Capital

✓ Physical Capital or Material Resources

✓ Money Capital or Monetary Resources, and

✓ Human Capital or Human Resources

11.6.1.1 Physical Capital

All man-made physical assets like plant and machinery, tools, buildings, roads, dams and communication, etc., are the various forms of physical capital.

11.6.1.1.1 Characteristics of Physical capital

✓ It is an asset which has a specific life period.

✓ Physical capital asset can be used in production again and again. As a result, it undergoes wear and tear or depreciation.

✓ When used in production, it gives a series of annual income flows called annuities, during its life period. Accumulation of more and more physical capital is called physical capital formation

11.6.1.2 Money Capital

The investment that is made in the form of money or monetary instruments is called money capital. A household saves its income in the form of bank deposits, shares and securities or other monetary instruments. These are the sources of money capital.

11.6.1.3 Human Capital

Human capital refers to the quality of labour resources, which can be improved through investments in education, training, and health. Higher the investments in human capital, higher will be the productivity.

11.6.2 Characteristics of capital

- ✓ Capital is a passive factor of production.
- ✓ Capital is man-made.
- ✓ Capital is not an indispensable factor of production, i.e. Production is possible even without capital.
- ✓ Capital has the highest mobility.
- ✓ Supply of capital is elastic.
- ✓ Capital is productive.
- ✓ Capital lasts over time (A plant may be in operation for a number of years).
- ✓ Capital involves present sacrifice (cost) to get future benefits.

Review of Questions

1. What is Production?
2. Define Capital?
3. Define Division of Labour.

Chapter: 12

Cost and Revenue

12.1 Cost

The concept of cost is used in variety of ways in economics. The term cost means expenses incurred in the production of a commodity. In simple language, the total amount of money spent on the production of a commodity is called cost. The various determinants of cost of production are the size of plant, the level of production, the nature of technology used, the quantity of inputs used, managerial and labour efficiency. Thus the cost of production of a commodity is the aggregate of prices paid for the factors of production used in producing a commodity.

12.2 Types of Cost

There are different types of cost which are as follow:

12.2.1 Money cost

The amount spent in terms of money for production of a commodity called money cost or nominal cost. It is the total money expenses incurred by a firm in producing a commodity. The term money cost includes Cost of raw materials, Wages and salaries of labour, Expenditure on machinery and equipment, Depreciation on machines, buildings and such other capital goods, Interest on capital, Other expenses like advertisement, insurance premium and taxes and Normal profit of the entrepreneur.

12.2.2 Real cost

Real cost is the pains and sacrifices involved in producing a commodity. The money paid for securing the factors of productions is money cost whereas the efforts and sacrifice made by the capitalists to save and invest, by the workers in foregoing leisure and by the landlords constitute real costs. In short, real cost is expressed not in money terms but in terms of efforts and sacrifices undergone in producing a commodity.

12.2.3 Opportunity Cost

The opportunity cost is the cost of next best alternatives foregone. In other words, it is the next best alternative good that is sacrificed. For example a farmer who is producing rice can produce onions with the same factors. Therefore the opportunity cost of a quintal of rice is the amount of output of onions given up.

12.2.4 Accounting Cost

Accounting costs are the payments made by the entrepreneur to the suppliers of various productive factors. It is also known as Explicit Cost. The accounting costs are only those costs, which are directly paid out or accounted for by the producer i.e. wages to the laborers employed, prices for the raw materials purchased, fuel and power used, rent for the building hired for the production work, the rate of interest on the borrowed capital and the taxes paid. Another name of it is direct Cost.

12.2.5 Economic cost

The economic cost includes not only the accounting cost but also the opportunity cost. The money rewards for the own services of the entrepreneur and the factors owned by himself and employed in production are known as implicit costs or imputed costs. The normal return on money capital invested by the entrepreneur, the wages or salary for his own services and rent of the land and buildings belonging to him and used in production constitute implicit cost.

Thus Economic cost = Explicit cost + Implicit cost.

12.2.6 Private cost

Private cost is the cost incurred by a firm for production. It includes both implicit costs and explicit costs.

12.2.7 Social Cost

Social costs are those costs, which are not borne by the producing firm but are incurred by others in society. For example, when an oil refinery discharges its waste in the river causing water pollution, such a pollution results in tremendous health hazards which involve costs to the society as a whole.

12.2.8 Fixed cost

The costs incurred on fixed factors are called fixed costs. Fixed costs are those which are independent of output, that is, they do not change with changes in output. These costs are a 'fixed' amount, which must be incurred by a firm in the short run whether the output is small or large. E.g. contractual rent, interest on capital invested, salaries to the permanent staff, insurance premier and certain taxes.

Variable Cost

The factors whose quantity can be changed in the short run are variable factors, and the costs incurred on variable factors are called variable costs. Variable costs are those costs, which are incurred on the employment of variable factors of production whose amount can be altered in the short run. Thus the total variable costs change with the level of output. It rises when output expands and falls when output contracts. When output is nil, variable cost becomes zero. These costs include payments such as wages of labour employed, prices of raw materials, fuel and power used and the transport costs.

12.2.9 Total cost

Total cost is the sum of total fixed cost and total variable cost.

$$TC = TFC + TVC \qquad \ldots (1)$$

Where

TC = Total cost

TC = Total Fixed cost

TVC = Total variable cost

It should be noted that total fixed cost is the same irrespective of the level of output. Therefore a change in total cost is influenced by the change in variable cost only.

12.2.10 Average Fixed Cost (AFC)

The average fixed cost is the fixed cost per unit of output. It is obtained by dividing the total fixed cost by the number of units of the commodity produced.

Symbolically AFC = TFC / Q   ... (2)

Where

AFC = Average fixed Cost

TFC = Total Fixed cost

Q = number of units of output produced

12.2.11   Average Variable cost (AVC)

Average variable cost is the variable cost per unit of output. It is the total variable cost divided by the number of units of output produced.

AVC = TVC / Q   ... (3)

Where

AVC = Average Variable Cost

TVC = Total Variable Cost

Q = number of units of output produced

Average variable cost curve is 'U' Shaped. As the output increases, the AVC will fall up to normal capacity output due to the operation of increasing returns. But beyond the normal capacity output, the AVC will rise due to the operation of diminishing returns.

12.2.12   Average Cost

Average total cost is simply called average cost which is the total cost divided by the number of units of output produced.

AC = TC / Q   ... (4)

Where

AC = Average Cost

TC = Total Cost

Q = number of units of output produced

Average cost is the sum of average fixed cost and average variable cost. i.e. AC = AFC+AVC

The average cost is also known as the unit cost since it is the cost per unit of output produced. AFC, AVC and ATC in the short period.

12.2.13   Marginal Cost

Marginal cost is defined as the addition made to the total cost by the production of one additional unit of output. Symbolically

$$MCn = TCn - TCn\text{-}1 \qquad \qquad \dots (5)$$

Where

MCn = Marginal cost

TC n = Total cost of producing n units

TC n-1 = Total cost of producing n-1 units

The marginal cost curve is 'U' shaped. The shape of the cost curve is determined by the law of variable proportions. If increasing returns is in operation, the marginal cost curve will be declining, as the cost will be decreasing with the increase in output. When the diminishing returns are in operation, the Marginal Cost curve will be increasing as it is the situation of increasing cost.

12.3 Cost function

The cost function expresses a functional relationship between costs and output that determine it. Symbolically, the cost function is

$$C = f(Q) \qquad \qquad \dots (6)$$

Where

C = Cost

Q = Output

12.4 REVENUE

The amount of money which the firm receives by the sale of its output in the market is known as its revenue. The Revenue of a firm is its sales, receipts or income.

12.5 Types of Revenue

There are different types of Revenue which are as follow:

12.5.1 Total Revenue

Total Revenue refers to the total amount of money that a firm receives from the sale of its products.

Mathematically TR = PQ where TR = Total Revenue; P = Price;

12.5.2 Average Revenue

Average revenue is the revenue per unit of the commodity sold. It is calculated by dividing the total revenue by the number of units sold.

$$AR = TR / Q \qquad \qquad ... (7)$$

Where AR = Average Revenue

TR = Total Revenue

Q = Quantity sold

Thus average revenue means price of the product.

12.5.3 Marginal Revenue

Marginal Revenue is the addition made to the total revenue by selling one more unit of a commodity.

$$\text{Mathematically } MR_n = TR_n - TR_{n-1} \qquad \qquad ... (8)$$

Review of Questions

1. What is Cost?

2. Define Revenue?

3. Define Marginal Cost.

4. Explain the types of Cost.

5. Describe the different types of Revenue.

Chapter: 13

Market

13.1 Market

In economics, the term market is used in a special sense. In the ordinary language, Market generally means a place or a geographical area, where buyers with money and sellers with their goods meet to exchange goods for money. However, In Economics, market refers to a group of buyers and sellers who involve in the transaction of commodities and services on not only any particular place but the entire area.

13.2 Features of a Market

The above definitions underline the following features of a Market:

✓ Existence of buyers and sellers of the commodity.

✓ The establishment of contact between the buyers and sellers. Distance is of no consideration if buyers and sellers could contact each other through the available communication system like telephone, agents, letter correspondence and Internet.

✓ Buyers and sellers deal with the same commodity or variety. Since the market in economics is identified on the basis of the commodity, similarity of the product is very essential.

✓ There should be a price for the commodity bought and sold in the market.

13.3 Types of Markets

A) Market according to Area

Based on the extent of the market for any product, markets can be classified into local regional, national and international markets.

1) **Local Market:** A local market for a product exists when buyers and sellers of commodity carry on business in a particular locality or village or area where the demand and supply conditions are influenced by local conditions only such as Perishable goods like milk and vegetables and bulky articles like bricks and stones.

2) **National Market:** When commodities are demanded and supplied throughout the country, there is national market such as wheat, rice or cotton markets

3) **Regional Market:** Commodities that are demanded and supplied over a region is regional market such as Tea market

4) **Global Market:** When demand and supply conditions are influenced at the global level such as gold, silver, cell phone

market is called Global Market. On the basis of demand and supply, this geographical classification is made. With improved transport facilities and communications, even goods of local markets can become international goods.

B) Market according to time

Marshall classified market based on the time element. In economics "time" does not mean clock time. It means only the division of time based on extent of adjustability of supply of a commodity for a given change in its demand. The major divisions are very short period, short period and long period.

1) **Very Short Period Market:** Very short period market refers to the type of competitive market in which the supply of commodities cannot be changed at all. So in a very short period, the market supply is perfectly inelastic. The price of the commodity depends on the demand for the product alone. The perishable commodities like flowers are the best example.

2) **Short-period Market:** Short period market refers to that period in which supply can be adjusted to a limited extent by varying the variable factors alone. The short period supply curve is relatively elastic. The short period price is determined by the interaction of the short-run supply and demand curves.

3) **Long Period Market:** Long period market is the time period during which the supply conditions are fully able to meet the new demand conditions. In the long run, all (both fixed as

well as variable) factors are variable. Thus the supply curve in the long run is perfectly elastic. Therefore, it is the demand that influences price in the long period.

C) Market according to competition

These markets are classified according to the number of sellers in the market and the nature of the commodity. The classification of market according to competition is as follows.

1) Perfect Competition

Perfect competition is a market situation where there is infinite number of sellers that no one is big enough to have any appreciable influence over market price. Thus Perfect Competition is that situation of the market wherein there are large numbers of buyers and sellers of a homogeneous product and the price of such a product is determined by the marker force, i.e., the industry.

Features of perfect competition

- ✓ There are a large number of buyers and sellers in a perfect competitive market that neither a single buyer nor a single seller can influence the price.
- ✓ The products produced by all the firms in the perfectly competitive market must be homogeneous and identical in all respects i.e. the products in the market are the same in quantity, size, taste, etc.
- ✓ Both buyers and sellers are fully aware of the current price in the market and having Perfect knowledge about market conditions.

- ✓ There must be complete freedom for the entry of new firms or the exit of the existing firms from the industry.

- ✓ The factors of productions should be free to move from one use to another or from one industry to another easily to get better remuneration.

- ✓ In a perfectly competitive market, it is assumed that there are no transport costs. Under perfect competition, a commodity is sold at uniform price throughout the market.

- ✓ There are no government controls or restrictions on supply, pricing etc.

Nature of Revenue curves

Under perfect competition, the market price is determined by the market forces namely the demand for and the supply of the products. Hence there is uniform price in the market and all the units of the output are sold at the same price. As a result the average revenue is perfectly elastic. The average revenue curve is horizontally parallel to X-axis. Since the Average Revenue is constant, Marginal Revenue is also constant and coincides with Average Revenue. AR curve of a firm represents the demand curve for the product produced by that firm.

Short run equilibrium price and output determination under perfect competition

- ✓ Since a firm in the perfectly competitive market is a price-taker, it has to adjust its level of output to maximize its profit. The aim of any producer is to maximize his profit.

- ✓ The short run is a period in which the number and plant size of the firms are fixed. In this period, the firm can produce more only by increasing the variable inputs.
- ✓ As the entry of new firms or exits of the existing firms are not possible in the short-run, the firm in the perfectly competitive market can either earn super-normal profit or normal profit or incur loss in the short period.

Super-normal Profit

When the average revenue of the firm is greater than its average cost, the firm is earning super-normal profit

Long run equilibrium, price and output determination

In the long run, all factors are variable. The firms can increase their output by increasing the number and plant size of the firms. Moreover, new firms can enter the industry and the existing firms can leave the industry. As a result, all the existing firms will earn only normal profit in the long run. If the existing firms earn supernormal profit, the new firms will enter the industry to compete with the existing firms. As a result, the output produced will increase. When the total output increases, the demand for factors of production will increase leading to increase in prices of the factors. This will result in increase in average cost. On the other side, when the output produced increases, the supply of the product increases. The demand remaining the same, when the supply of the product increases, the price of the product comes down. Hence the average revenue will come down. A fall in average revenue and the rise in average cost will continue till both become equal. (AR = AC). Thus, all the perfectly competitive firms will earn normal profit in the long run.

Advantages of perfect competition

- ✓ There is consumer sovereignty in a perfect competitive market. The consumer is rational and he has perfect knowledge about the market conditions. Therefore, he will not purchase the products at a higher price.

- ✓ In the perfectly competitive market, the price is equal to the minimum average cost. It is beneficial to the consumer.

- ✓ The perfectly competitive firms are price-takers and the products are homogeneous. Therefore it is not necessary for the producers to incur expenditure on advertisement to promote sales. This reduces the wastage of resources.

- ✓ In the long run, the perfectly competitive firm is functioning at the optimum level. This means that maximum economic efficiency in production is achieved. As the actual output produced by the firm is equal to the optimum output, there is no idle or unused or excess capacity.

2) **Monopoly**

Monopoly is a market structure in which there is a single seller, there are no close substitutes for the commodity it produces and there are barriers to entry.

Features of Monopoly

- ✓ There is only one seller; he can control either price or supply of his product. But he cannot control demand for the product, as there are many buyers.

- ✓ There are no close substitutes for the product. The buyers have no alternatives or choice. Either they have to buy the product or go without it.

- ✓ The monopolist has control over the supply so as to increase the price. Sometimes he may adopt price discrimination. He may fix different prices for different sets of consumers. A monopolist can either fix the price or quantity of output; but he cannot do both, at the same time.

- ✓ There is no freedom to other producers to enter the market as the monopolist is enjoying monopoly power. There are strong barriers for new firms to enter. There are legal, technological, economic and natural obstacles, which may block the entry of new producers.

- ✓ Under monopoly, there is no difference between a firm and an industry. As there is only one firm, that single firm constitutes the whole industry. .

Causes for Monopoly

- ✓ **Natural:** A monopoly may arise on account of some natural causes. Some minerals are available only in certain regions. For example, South Africa has the monopoly of diamonds; nickel in the world is mostly available in Canada and oil in Middle East. This is natural monopoly.

- ✓ **Technical**: Monopoly power may be enjoyed due to technical reasons. A firm may have control over raw materials, technical knowledge, special know-how, scientific secrets and formula that enable a monopolist to produce a commodity. e.g., Coco Cola.

- ✓ **Legal:** Monopoly power is achieved through patent rights, copyright and trade marks by the producers. This is called legal monopoly.

- ✓ **Large Amount of Capital**: The manufacture of some goods requires a large amount of capital or lumpiness of capital. All firms cannot enter the field because they cannot afford to invest such a large amount of capital. This may give rise to monopoly. For example, iron and steel industry, railways, etc.

- ✓ **State:** Government will have the sole right of producing and selling some goods. They are State monopolies. For example, we have public utilities like electricity and railways. These public utilities are undertaken by the State.

Price and Output Determination

A monopolist like a perfectly competitive firm tries to maximize his profits. A monopoly firm faces a downward sloping demand curve, that is, its average revenue curve. The downward sloping demand curve implies that larger output can be sold only by reducing the price. Its marginal revenue curve will be below the average revenue curve. The average cost curve is 'U' shaped. The monopolist will be in equilibrium when MC = MR and the MC curve cuts the MR curve from below.

Advantages

- ✓ Monopoly firms have large-scale production possibilities and also can enjoy both internal and external economies. This will result in the reduction of costs of production. Output can be sold at low prices. This is beneficial to the consumers.

- ✓ Monopoly firms have vast financial resources which could be used for research and development. This will enable the firms to innovate quickly.

- ✓ There are a number of weak firms in an industry. These firms can combine together in the form of monopoly to meet competition. In such a case, market can be expanded. Although there are some advantages, there is a danger that monopoly power might be misused for exploiting the consumers.

Disadvantages

- ✓ A monopolist always charges a high price, which is higher than the competitive price. Thus a monopolist exploits the consumers.

- ✓ A monopolist is interested in getting maximum profit. He may restrict the output and raise prices. Thus, he creates artificial scarcity for his product.

- ✓ A monopolist often charges different prices for the same product from different consumers. He extracts maximum price according to the ability to pay of different consumers.

- ✓ A monopolist uses large-scale production and huge resources to promote his own selfish interest. He may adopt wrong practices to establish absolute monopoly power.

- ✓ In a country dominated by monopolies, wealth is concentrated in the hands of a few. It will lead to inequality of incomes. This is against the principle of the socialistic pattern of society.

Methods of Controlling Monopoly

- ✓ **Legislative Method:** Government can control monopolies by legal actions. Anti-monopoly legislation has been enacted to check the growth of monopoly. In India, the Monopolies and Restrictive Trade Practices Act was passed in 1969. The objective of this Act is to prevent the unwanted growth of private monopolies and concentration of economic power in the hands of a small number of individuals and families.

- ✓ **Controlling Price and Output:** This method can be applied in the case of natural monopolies. Government would fix either price or output or both.

- ✓ **Taxation:** Taxation is another method by which the monopolistic power can be prevented or restricted. Government can impose a lump-sum tax on a monopoly firm, irrespective of its level of output. Consequently, its total profit will fall.

- ✓ **Nationalization:** Nationalizing big companies is one of the solutions. Government may take over such monopolistic companies, which are exploiting the consumers.

- ✓ **Consumer's Association**: The growth of monopoly power can also be controlled by encouraging the formation of consumers associations to improve the bargaining power of consumers.

3) Price Discrimination

Price discrimination means the practice of selling the same commodity at different prices to different buyers. If the monopolist charges different prices from different consumers for the same commodity, it is called price discrimination or discriminating monopoly. Thus, Price discrimination occurs when the same commodity is sold at more than one price. A monopolist often charges different price of a same product from different consumers or different industries. This is also known as Discriminating Monopolist.

Definition

Price discrimination may be defined as *"the sale of technically similar products at prices which are not proportional to marginal cost"*. For example, all cinema theatres charge different prices for different classes of people.

Conditions of Price Discrimination

Price discrimination is possible only if the following conditions are fulfilled.

✓ The demand must not be transferable from the high priced market to the low priced market. If rich people do not buy the high-priced deluxe edition of the book, but wait for the low-priced popular edition to come out, then personal discrimination will fail.

✓ The monopolist should keep the two markets or different markets separate so that the commodity will not be moving from one market to the other market. If it is possible to buy the product in the cheaper market of the monopolist and sell it in the dearer market, there can never be two prices for the commodity. If the industrial buyer of cheap electricity uses it for domestic consumption, then trade discrimination will fail. The above two conditions are essential to adopt price discrimination.

4) Monopolistic Competition

Monopolistic competition, as the name itself implies, is a blending of monopoly and competition. Monopolistic competition refers to the market situation in which a large number of sellers produce goods which are close substitutes of one another. The products are similar but not identical. The particular brand of product will have a group of loyal consumers. In this respect, each firm will have some monopoly and at the same time the firm has to compete in the market with the other firms as they produce a fair substitute. The essential features of monopolistic competition are product differentiation and existence of many sellers.

Features of Monopolistic Competition

✓ Monopolistic competition, the number of firms producing a commodity will be very large. The term 'very large' denotes that contribution of each firm towards the total demand of the product is small. Each firm will act independently on the basis of product differentiation and each firm determines its price-output policies. Any action of the individual firm in increasing or decreasing the output will have little or no effect on other firms.

✓ Product differentiation is the essence of monopolistic competition. Product differentiation is the process of altering goods that serve the same purpose so that they differ in minor ways.

✓ From the discussion of 'product differentiation', we can infer that the producer under monopolistic competition has to incur expenses to popularize his brand. This expenditure involved in selling the product is called selling cost. According to Prof. Chamberlin, selling cost is "the cost incurred in order to alter the position or shape of the demand curve for a product". Most important form of selling cost is advertisement. Sales promotion by advertisement is called non-price competition.

✓ Another important feature is the freedom of any firm to enter into the field and produce the commodity under its own brand name and any firm can go out of the field if so chosen. There are no barriers as in the case of monopoly Monopolistic competition presupposes that customers have definite preferences for particular varieties or brand of products.

Determination of Equilibrium price and output under monopolistic competition

The monopolistic competitive firm will come to equilibrium on the principle of equalizing MR with MC. Each firm will choose that price and output where it will be maximizing its profit.

Equilibrium of the individual firm in the short period.

The different firms in monopolistic competition may be making either abnormal profits or losses in the short period depending on their costs and revenue curves. In the long run, if the existing firms earn super normal profit, the entry of new firms will reduce its share in the market. The average revenue of the product will come down. The demand for factors of production will increase the cost of production. Hence, the size of the profit will be reduced. If the existing firms incur losses in the long-run, some of the firms will leave the industry increasing the share of the existing firms in the market. Thus under monopolistic competition, all the existing firms will earn normal profit in the long run.

Disadvantages of Monopolistic competition

- ✓ Under monopolistic competition, the firms produce less than optimum output. As a result, the productive capacity is not used to the fullest extent. This will lead to unemployment of resources.

- ✓ Excess capacity is the difference between the optimum output that can be produced and the actual output produced by the firm. In the long run, a monopolistic firm produces an output which is less than the optimum output that is the output corresponding to the minimum average cost. This leads to excess capacity which is regarded as waste in monopolistic competition.

✓ There is a lot of waste in competitive advertisements under monopolistic competition. The wasteful and competitive advertisements lead to high cost to consumers.

✓ Introducing too many varieties of a good is another waste of monopolistic competition. The goods differ in size, shape, style and color. A reasonable number of varieties would be desirable. Cost per unit can be reduced if only a few are produced.

✓ Under monopolistic competition, inefficient firms charge prices higher than their marginal cost. Such type of inefficient firms should be kept out of the industry. But, the buyers' preference for such products enables the inefficient firms to continue to exist. Efficient firms cannot drive out the inefficient firms because the former may not be able to attract the customers of the latter.

5) Oligopoly

Oligopoly refers to a form of imperfect competition where there will be only a few sellers producing either homogenous or differentiated products.

Features of Oligopoly

✓ The most important feature of oligopoly is interdependence in decision - making. Since there are a few firms, each firm closely watches the activities of the other firm. Any change in price, output, product, etc., by a firm will have a direct effect on the fortune of its rivals. So an oligopolistic firm must consider not only the market demand for its product, but also the possible moves of other firms in the industry.

✓ Firms may realize the importance of mutual co-operation. Then they will have a tendency of collusion. At the same time, the desire of each firm to earn maximum profit may encourage competitive spirit. Thus, co-operative and collusive trend as well as competitive trend would prevail in an oligopolistic market.

✓ Another important feature of oligopoly is price rigidity. Price is sticky or rigid at the prevailing level due to the fear of reaction from the rival firms. If an oligopolistic firm lowers its price, the price reduction will be followed by the rival firms. As a result, the firm loses its profit. Expecting the same kind of reaction, if the oligopolistic firm raises the price, the rival firms will not follow. This would result in losing customers. In both ways the firm would face difficulties. Hence the price is rigid.

Review of Questions

1. What is Market?
2. Define Perfect Competition?
3. Define Monopoly.
4. Explain the Oligopoly.
5. Describe the Monopolistic Competition.

Chapter: 14

Income Distribution

In order to produce goods and services in each country every year, there is need of factor of production like land, labour, capital and entrepreneur. The price which is paid to these factors for their services is called factor price such as wages to labour, interest to capital, rent to land and profit to entrepreneur. In this ways, income distribution is therefore concerned with the determination of prices of the services of different factor of production.

14.1 Rent

In simple language, Rent refers to any periodic payment made for the use of a good. For example, when we live in someone's house, we pay rent. This rent is contract payment. The contract rent includes besides the payment made for the use of land, interest on the capital invested in the house, wages and profit. But classical economists like Ricardo referred by Rent to the payment made for the use of agricultural land. Rent arises because of the peculiar characteristics of land. The supply of land is inelastic and it differs in fertility. Rent arises because of differences in fertility. Those lands which are more fertile than others get rent.

14.1.1 The Ricardian theory of Rent

Ricardian theory of rent is one of the earliest theories of rent. It is named after Ricardo, a great classical economist of the 19th century. According to Ricardo, "rent is that portion of the produce of the earth which is paid to the landlord for the use of the original and indestructible powers of the soil". So rent is payment made for the use of land for its original powers. Ricardo believed that rent arose on account of differences in the fertility of land. Only superior lands get rent. Rent is a differential surplus. Rent may also arise on account of situational advantage. For example, some lands may be nearer to the market. The producer can save a lot of transport costs. Even if all lands are equally fertile, lands which enjoy situational advantage will earn rent. Ricardo explained his theory by taking the example of colonization. If some people go and settle down in a place, first they will cultivate the best lands. If more people go and settle down, the demand for land will increase and they will cultivate the second-grade lands. The cost of production will go up. So the price of grain in the market must cover the cost of cultivation. In this case, the first grade land will get rent. After some time, if there is increase in population, even third grade lands will be cultivated. Now, even second grade lands will get rent and first grade lands will get more rent but the third grade land will not get rent. It is known as no - rent land. According to Ricardo, rent is price determined, that is, it is determined by price of the grains produced in the land. He also believed that rent is high because price is high and not the other way round. Ricardo came to the conclusion that rent did not enter price because there are some no - rent or marginal lands. As the produce of no-rent land gets a price, Ricardo argued that rent did not enter price.

Criticism of the Ricardian Theory of Rent

Ricardo tells that only the best lands are cultivated first. There is no historical proof for this.

- ✓ According to Ricardo, land has "original and indestructible powers". But the fertility of land may decline after some time because of continuous cultivation.
- ✓ Ricardo believed that rent is peculiar to land alone. But many modern economists argue that the rent aspect can be seen in other factors like labour and capital. Rent arises whenever the supply of a factor is inelastic in relation to the demand for it.
- ✓ Ricardo is of the view that rent does not enter the price of the commodity produced in it. But rent enters the price from the point of view of a single firm.
- ✓ Ricardian theory does not take note of scarcity rent.
- ✓ It is based on perfect competition. Only under perfect competition, there will be one price for a good. But in the real world, we have imperfect competition. Though there are some criticisms against the Ricardian theory, we may note it

tells that because of increasing pressure on land, we have to cultivate inferior lands.

14.1.2 Modern Theory of Rent

In the modern theory of rent, the term rent refers to "payments made for factors of production which are in imperfectly elastic supply". By this definition, rent is applied to other factors like labour and capital. In other words, rent does not apply to land alone. Just as land differs in fertility, men differ in their ability. For example, a surgeon with a rare skill may earn a lot of income. There is an element of rent in it. In fact, we have a theory of profits known as "Rent theory of profits". Marshall has introduced the concept of "Quasi-rent" with regard to machines and other man-made appliances. So the modern view is that rent can be applied to all factors of production. Whenever, the supply of a factor is inelastic in relation to the demand for it, rent arises. To explain rent, modern economists also make use of the term transfer earnings. Transfer earnings refer to the amount that a factor could earn in its best paid alternative employment. It represents the opportunity cost of its present employment. Any payment in excess of this amount is a surplus above what is necessary to retain the factor in its best-paid employment and so is rent. Thus, any payment in excess of transfer earnings is economic rent. If a popular south Indian Cinema actor who is normally paid, say Rs.two crores, gets an offer to act in a Hindi film for Rs. three corers, his transfer earnings are Rs. two crores. Rs. one crore may be considered as economic rent for acting in the Hindi film. So the main point about the modern theory of rent is that rent is not peculiar to land alone. The rent aspect can be seen in other factor incomes as well.

14.1.3 Quasi-Rent

According to Marshall, 'Quasi-rent is the income derived from machines and other appliances for production by man". There are some machines and other man-made appliances (e.g. boats) whose supply may be inelastic in the short run in relation to the demand for them. For example, when there is large increase in demand for fish during a season, the demand for boats will increase. But you cannot increase their supply over night. So they will earn some extra income over and above the normal income they receive. This, Marshall calls Quasi-rent. Quasi-rent will disappear, when once the supply of boats increases.

14.2 Wages

Wages are the reward for labour. There are two main kinds of wages. (1) Money wages and (2) Real wages. Money wages are also known as nominal wages. Real wages refer to the commodities and services which the money wages command. They depend mainly on the purchasing power of money, which in turn depends upon the price level. The standard of living of workers in a country depends upon the real wages. Further, a farm worker may get low money wages. But if he gets free board and lodging, we must take that also into account while considering real wages.

14.2.1 Theories of wages

There are many theories of wages. Some of the early theories of wages are: 1. The Subsistence Theory of wages ; 2. The Standard

128

of Living Theory ; 3. The Wages Fund Theory ; 4. The Residual Claimant Theory

Some of the important recent theories of wages are

- ✓ The Marginal productivity theory of wages;
- ✓ The Market theory of wages and
- ✓ The Bargaining theory of wages.

14.2.2 Early theories of wages

- ✓ **The subsistence theory of Wages:** According to this theory, the wages that are paid to a worker must be just enough to cover his bare needs of subsistence. If the workers are paid less than the subsistence wage, there will be starvation and death and it will result in shortage of supply of labour. The main criticism against the theory is that it is based on the assumption that an increase in wages will result in an increase in population. Man is different from an animal. Besides bare needs, he needs some comforts. This theory does not take note of that. And it is one sided. It ignores the forces operating on the side of demand. This theory is based on bad ethics.

- ✓ **The standard of living theory:** This theory tells that wages depend upon the standard of living of workers. There is no doubt that the standard of living theory is an improvement on the subsistence theory. It is true that there is relationship between standard of living and wages. But it is rather difficult to say which the cause is and which is the result.

- ✓ **The Wages Fund Theory:** According to Wages Fund Theory, "wages depend upon the proportion between population and capital". The term "capital" in the context refers to the fund set apart for payment of wages. And the word 'population' refers to workers. If the supply of workers increases, wages will fall and vice versa. This theory can be criticized because this theory assumes that an increase in wages will result in an increase in population. But there is no direct relationship between the two. Further, it tells that if wages rise, profits will fall. This is not correct because during periods of good trade, both wages and profits will rise.

- ✓ **The Residual Claimant Theory:** According to this theory, wages "equal the whole product minus rent, interest and profits" (Walker). In other words, the theory tells that wages are paid out of the residue that is left over after making payment for rent, interest and profits. The main criticism against the theory is that it considers wages as residual payment. But wages are in the nature of advance payment and they have to be paid first. Normally, profits are taken at the end.

14.2.3 Recent Theories of wages

- ✓ **The Marginal productivity theory of wages:** The marginal productivity theory of wages is only an application of the marginal productivity theory of distribution, which is a general theory of distribution. The theory explains how wages are determined under conditions of perfect competition. According to the marginal productivity theory, wages will be equal to the value of the marginal product of labour. As an employer goes on employing more and more units of labour, its marginal product will fall because of the law of diminishing marginal returns. So he will employ labour up to the point where the wages he pays are equal to the value of the marginal product of labour. All units are assumed to be uniform. So the productivity of the marginal unit of labor determines the rate at which wages are to be paid to all units of labour. This theory can be criticized because :1. Every product is produced by the joint effort of all factors of production. It is rather difficult to measure the productivity of each factor in terms of the product produced. The difficulty is more in measuring the marginal productivity of those who render services (eg. doctors, actors and lawyers); 2. it is based on the assumption of perfect competition. But in the real world, we have only imperfect competition ; 3) under monopoly, wages will be lower than the marginal product of labour because there is exploitation of labour ; 4) wages are in the nature of advance payment. So an employer will deduct some amount to cover the interest on capital and pay the workers' wages which are lower than their marginal product. So wages are the discounted marginal product of labour 5). The theory should not be used to justify the low wages in an economy and the inequalities of incomes. Wages might be low because of exploitation of labour. In spite of the above criticism, "the doctrine throws into clear light the action of one of the causes that govern wages". (Marshall).

✓ **The Market Theory of Wages:** The market theory looks at wages as the price of labour. Like all other prices, wages are determined by the market forces of supply and demand. The supply of labour generally refers to the total number of people available for employment. Some types of labour require long periods of training. During that long period, workers have to sacrifice their earnings. We have to take note of the foregone earnings while estimating the cost of labour which determines its supply.

✓ **The Bargaining Theory of Wages:** The bargaining theory of wages takes note of the influence of trade unions on wages through collective bargaining. According to the theory, the level of wages in an industry depends on the bargaining strength of the trade union concerned. The strength of a trade union depends upon many things like the size of its membership, the size of its "fighting fund", and its ability to cause dislocation in the industry and the economy through strike. During periods of full employment and good trade, trade unions will be in a strong position and during depression marked by bad trade and mass unemployment; trade unions will be in a weak position. A trade union may increase wages by restricting the supply of labour. For example, it may insist that only members of a trade union

132

should be employed. This is known as closed shop policy. It may threaten that it will go on strike if a minimum wage is not paid.

14.3 Interest

Interest is the price paid for the use of capital. This is 'net interest' or 'pure interest'. A good example of pure interest is the interest we get on some government securities. It may be regarded as net interest. Gross interest, includes besides net interest, other things such as reward for risk, remuneration for inconvenience and payment for services. Thus gross interest covers trade risks and personal risks. For example, when a money lender lends money to an Indian farmer, he charges high rate of interest because there is the risk of non - payment of the amount borrowed. There are trade risks and personal risks. Generally, people prefer to have cash balances. This is known as liquidity preference. When you lend money to someone, you cannot get it for some time. And that is inconvenience. So to compensate it, one must be paid some extra income. So, gross interest includes compensation for all the above things besides net interest.

14.3.1 Theories of Interest

Some of the theories of interest are (1) The Abstinence or Waiting Theory of Interest; 2. The Agio Theory and Time Preference Theory; 3. The Marginal Productivity Theory; 4. Saving and Investment Theory (The classical theory) 5. Loanable Funds Theory and 6. The Liquidity Preference Theory

According to the Abstinence theory of Nassau Senior, interest is the reward for abstaining from the immediate consumption of wealth,. When people save, they abstain from present consumption. That involves some sacrifice. To make them save, interest is offered as a reward. But Marshall preferred the word, "waiting" to "abstinences". The "Agio"theory of interest of Bohm-Bawerk tells that as the present carries a premium (agio) over the future, and as people prefer present consumption to future consumption, we have to pay a price for them by way of compensation. And that is interest. The time preference theory of Irving Fisher is more or less the same as Agio theory of interest. The marginal productivity theory of distribution is nothing but the application of the marginal productivity theory of distribution. It tells that interest tends to equal the marginal productivity of capital. The classical theory of interest tells that the rate of interest is determined by the supply of capital which depends upon savings and the demand for capital for investment. The theory is based on the assumption that there is a direct relationship between the rate of interest, savings and direct relationship between interest and investment. The

Classical economists believed that savings would increase when the interest rates were high, and investment would increase with a fall in interest rate. And the equilibrium between saving and investment was brought about by the rate of interest.

14.3.2 Loanable funds theory (Neo – classical theory) of Interest

The Loanable funds theory was developed by Knut Wicksell, Dennis Robertson and others. The Loanable funds theory is wider in its scope than the classical theory of interest. The term "Loanable funds" includes not only saving out of current income but also bank credit, dishoarding and disinvestments. But by saving, the classical economists referred only to saving out of current income. We know now that bank credit is an important source of funds for investment. In the classical theory, saving was demanded only for investment. But according to Loanable funds theory, the demand for funds arose, not only for investment but also for hoarding wealth. The classical theory regarded interest as a function of saving and investment, (r = f (S.I.) But, according to Loanable funds theory, the rate of interest is a function of four variables, i.e.

$$r = f (1, S M.L.) \qquad\qquad ... (1)$$

Where

r is the rate of interest, I = investment, S = saving, M = bank credit and

L = desire to hoard or the desire for liquidity.

Criticism: There is no doubt that Loanable funds theory is an improvement over the classical theory of interest. It has been criticized on the ground that it assumes that saving is a function of the rate of interest; 2. it ignores the influence of the changes in the level of investment on employment, income and on savings.

14.3.3 Liquidity preference theory (Keynesian theory) of interest.

Generally people prefer to hold a part of their assets in the form of cash. Cash is a liquid asset. According to Keynes, interest is the reward for parting with liquidity for a specified period of time. In other words, it is the reward for not hoarding. According to Keynes, people have liquidity preference for three motives. They are 1. Transaction motive; 2. Precautionary motive; and 3. Speculative motive. The transaction motive refers to the money held to finance day to

day spending. Precautionary money is held to meet an unforeseen expenditure. Keynes defines speculative motive as "the object of securing profit from knowing better than the market what the future will bring forth." Of the three motives, speculative motive is more important in determining the rate of interest. Keynes believed that the amount of money held for speculative motive would vary inversely with the rate of interest. Keynes was of the view that the rate of interest was determined by liquidity preference on the one hand and the supply of money on the

other. This theory can be criticized because Keynesian theory is a general theory of interest and it is far superior to the earlier theories of interest. But critics say that Keynes has over - emphasized liquidity preference factor in the theory of interest. Moreover, only when a person has savings, the question of parting with liquidity arises. In the words of Jacob Viner, "without saving, there can be no liquidity to surrender. The rate of interest is the return for "saving without liquidity".

14.4 Profits

Profits are the reward for organization or entrepreneurship. Risk taking and uncertainty-bearing are the main functions of an entrepreneur. So we may consider profit as the reward for the above functions.

14.4.1 Types of Profits

Different Types of Profit is given as follow:

- ✓ **Gross Profit and Net Profit:** Generally when we speak of profit, we refer to the difference between the total expenses of producing a good and the total revenue from it. But this is gross profit. Gross profit includes besides net profit other things such as the interest on capital, rent of land, wages of management and some extra income on account of the monopoly position of a firm. It also includes some chance gains (windfall profits). While considering net profit 'or' pure profit, we have to deduct all the above things from gross profit. Net profit is the reward for risk – taking and uncertainty - bearing which are the main functions of an entrepreneur. The monopolist is the sole seller of a commodity for which there are no substitutes. As he controls the supply, it is possible for him to make huge profits. And this is known as monopoly profit.

- ✓ **Normal profit and super normal profit:** Pure profit (net profit) can be divided into normal profit and supernormal profit. Normal profit is the minimum necessary to guarantee that an entrepreneur will continue to bear uncertainty and run the firm. That part of pure profit which is in excess of normal profit is excess or surplus profit or supernormal profit. Though firms under perfect competition may make surplus profits in the short run, it will disappear in the long run. Only a monopoly can earn excess profits indefinitely. The early economists made no distinction between interest and profits because they considered the capitalist and the entrepreneur as one and the same person. The entrepreneur need not necessarily be the owner of capital. It is leadership rather than ownership that is important in the case of an entrepreneur. Today, organization has become a distinct factor of production. Profits differ from other incomes in three ways. First, it is a residual income. Second, there may be wide fluctuations in profits and sometimes, they may be negative. That is, there may be losses. We cannot think of negative wages. Third, profits are uncertain.

14.4.2 Theories of Profit

Some of the important theories of profit are (1) the rent theory of profits (2) The marginal productivity theory of profits; (3) The wages theory of profits; (4) the dynamic theory of profits; (5) the innovation theory of profits (6) the risk theory of profits, and (7) the uncertainty – bearing theory of profits.

14.4.2.1 Rent theory of profits

- ✓ **Prof Walker** is the author of the rent theory of profits. In his view, profits are the "rent of ability" and they are similar to rent. Rent arises because of differences in fertility of land. Similarly profits arise because of differences in ability. That is why it is called the "rent of ability". The main criticism against this theory is that it explains only why there are differences in profits. It does not answer the fundamental question why there are profits as such.

- ✓ **The Marginal productivity theory of Profits:** The theory is an application of the general theory of distribution. According to this theory, under perfect competition, profits will be equal to the value of the marginal product of organization. We can apply all the criticisms against marginal productivity theory to this theory also.

- ✓ **The wages theory of Profits:** According to Prof. Taussig, profits are not different from wages. Profits are the wages of the entrepreneur for his special ability. Profits are the wages of management. The criticism against the theory is that we can speak of negative profits (losses) but we cannot speak of negative wages. Organization is a distinct factor of production. And it is different from labour.

- ✓ **The Dynamic Theory of profits:** Prof. Clark is the author of this theory. According to him, profits are the result of dynamic changes in society. Clark has defined profits as the excess of the prices of goods over their costs. Some of the important changes relate to the size of population, supply of capital, production techniques, industrial organization and human wants. Though the dynamic theory is one of the modern theories of profits, "it overlooks the fundamental question of the difference between a change that is foreseen a reasonable time in advance and one that is unforeseen".

- ✓ **Innovation theory of profits:** According to Schumpeter, profits are the reward for innovations. An innovation is something more than an invention. An invention becomes an innovation only when it is applied to industrial processes. Innovation includes introduction of new goods, or new methods of production and opening new market. And innovations are introduced by the entrepreneur. Change and economic development take place because of his activities. So he gets profits for innovations. The criticism against the theory is that though innovation is an important factor in the emergence of profits, it cannot be the only factor. It ignores the risk-bearing function of the entrepreneur.

- ✓ **The Risk - bearing theory of profits:** According to Prof. Hawley, profits are the reward for an entrepreneur for risk-taking. Risk - taking is an important function of an entrepreneur. Risk-taking and profit-making go together. The main criticism against this theory is that it does not make distinction between known risks and unknown risks. Known risks (eg. theft, fire) can be insured against. We may say that profits are the reward for taking unknown risks. For there is a lot of uncertainty about such risks.

- ✓ **The uncertainty-bearing theory of profits:** Professor Knight is the author of the uncertainty - bearing theory of profits. He is of the view that "profit is the reward not for risk - bearing but uncertainty bearing". His main point is that there is risk because future is uncertain. And uncertainty -

bearing is an essential function of an entrepreneur. The entrepreneur can insure known risks. But unknown risks (eg. competition risks, risks of government action) cannot be insured against. These risks are uncertain. The entrepreneur earns profits because uncertainties are borne by him. The criticism against the theory is that uncertainty - bearing alone is not the only function of an entrepreneur.

Conclusion: The main defect with all the above theories is that they stress only one or two functions of the entrepreneur. In addition to risk-taking and uncertainty-bearing, the entrepreneur performs a number of other functions. And he deserves reward in the form of profits.

14.5 The marginal productivity theory of distribution

The marginal productivity theory of distribution is the general theory of income distribution. The theory explains how prices of various factors of production are determined under conditions of perfect competition. It emphasizes that any variable factor must obtain a reward equal to its marginal product. Factor prices are determined in markets under the forces of supply and demand. But there is one difference. While the demand for commodities is direct demand, the demand for factors of production is derived demand. Though the theory is applicable to all factors of production, we may illustrate it with reference to labour. A firm will go on employing more and more units of a factor until the price of that factor is equal to the value of the marginal product. In other words, each factor will be rewarded according to its marginal productivity. The marginal productivity is equal to the value of the additional product which an employer gets when he employs an additional unit of that factor. We assume that the supply of all other factors remain constant. We shall give a simple illustration of the marginal productivity theory of distribution by making use of labour. The aim of a firm is maximization of profit. It will hire a factor as long as it adds more to total revenue than to total cost. Thus a firm will hire a factor up to the point at which the marginal unit contributes as much to total cost as to total revenue because total profit cannot be further increased. It is assumed that a firm can employ any amount of labour under a given wage rate as the supply of labour is assumed to be unlimited in a competitive market.

The condition of equilibrium in the labour market is

$$MCL = VMPL \qquad \ldots (2)$$

Where MCL = Marginal cost of labour

VMPL = Value of marginal product of labour.

$$Or \; W = VMPL \qquad \ldots (3)$$

Where W = wages of labour

MPPL = Marginal physical product (of labour) curve

VMPL = Value of marginal product curve

VMPL = MPPL.PX (VMPL = Marginal physical product of labour multiplied by price of the commodity)

P (The price is assumed to be constant under conditions of perfect competition)

Thus the productivity of the marginal unit of a factor determines the rate that is to be paid to all units of the factor. The employer adopts the principle of substitution and combines land, labour and capital in such a way that the cost of production is minimum. Then the reward for each factor is determined by its marginal productivity. The marginal productivity theory of distribution has been used to explain the determination of rent, wages, interest and profits. That is why; it is called general theory of distribution.

Assumptions of the theory

The marginal productivity theory is based on the following assumptions.

- ✓ There is perfect competition.
- ✓ All units of a factor are homogeneous. It means that one unit of a factor is the same as the other.
- ✓ Factors can be substituted for each other. That is, all factors are interchangeable.
- ✓ The theory is based on the law of diminishing returns as applied to business. The law of diminishing returns tells that if you go on employing more and more units of a factor, its marginal returns will diminish. So a firm, when it comes to know that the increase in a certain factor is resulting in diminishing returns, the firm will substitute it with some other factor. Thereby, it will try to reduce the cost of production.

Criticism of the theory

The following are some of the points of criticism against the marginal productivity theory of distribution.

- ✓ Every product is a joint product and its value cannot be separately attributed to either labour or capital. Again, it is rather difficult to measure the "productivity" of certain categories of labour like doctors, lawyers and teachers who render services.

- ✓ The theory takes into account only the factors operating on the side of demand by ignoring the supply side. For example, when there is scarcity of a factor, it is paid much more than the normal price.

- ✓ The theory is based on the assumption of perfect competition and full employment. But in the real world, we have only imperfect competition; we do not have perfect competition.

- ✓ In practice, it is rather difficult to vary the use of the factors of production.

- ✓ The theory does not carry with it any ethical justification. If we accept the theory, it means that factors get the value of what they produce. For example, workers in a firm may get low wages not because their productivity is low but because there might be exploitation of labour. Hence we should not make use of this theory to justify the existing system of unequal distribution. We may note that in spite of the above points of criticism against the theory, it explains the role of productivity in the determination of factor prices. In the words of Marshall, "the doctrine throws into clear light one of the causes that govern wages".

Review of Questions

1. What is Rent?

2. Define Wages?

3. Define Profit.

4. Explain the Ricardian theory of Rent.

5. Describe the marginal productivity theory of distribution.

Chapter: 15

Entrepreneurs

15.1 Entrepreneurship

An entrepreneur is a person who combines the different factors of production (land, labour and capital), in the right proportion and initiates the process of production and also bears the risk involved in it. The entrepreneur is also called 'organizer'. Entrepreneurship is risk taking, managerial, and organizational skills needed to produce goods and services in order to gain a profit. In modern times, an entrepreneur is called 'the changing agent of the society'. He is not only responsible for producing the socially desirable output but also to increase the social welfare. Thus, Entrepreneurs are Human who has the personality of business activities with focus on achieving their physical and financial targets

15.2 Functions of an Entrepreneur

A function of an Entrepreneur is as follows:

- ✓ **Identifying Profitable Investible Opportunities**

  Conceiving a new and most promising and profitable idea or capturing a new idea available in the market is the foremost function of an entrepreneur. This is known as identifying profitable investible opportunities.

✓ **Deciding the size of unit of production**

An entrepreneur has to decide the size of the unit – whether big or small depending upon the nature of the product and the level of competition in the market.

✓ **Deciding the location of the production unit**

A rational entrepreneur will always locate his unit of production nearer to both factor market and the end-use market. This is to be done in order to bring down the delay in production and distribution of products and to reduce the storage and transportation cost.

✓ **Identifying the optimum combination of factors of production**

The entrepreneur, after having decided to start a new venture, takes up the task of hiring factors of production. Further, he decides in what combinations he should combine these factors so that maximum output is produced at minimum cost.

✓ **Making innovations**

According to Schumpeter, basically an entrepreneur is an innovator of new markets and new techniques of production. A new market increases the sales volume whereas a new cost cutting production technique will make the product cheaper. This will in turn increase the volume of sales and the profit.

6) **Deciding the reward payment**

The factors used in production have to be rewarded on the basis of their productivity. Measuring the productivity of the factors and the payment of reward is the crucial function of an entrepreneur.

7) **Taking Risks and facing uncertainties**

According to Hawley, a business is nothing but a bundle of risks. Products are produced for future demand. The future is uncertain. The investments are made in the present. This is the serious risk in production. One who is ready to accept the risk becomes a successful entrepreneur. A prudent entrepreneur forecasts the future risks scientifically and take appropriate decision in the present to overcome such risks. According to Knight one of the important functions of entrepreneur is uncertainty bearing.

Review of Questions

1. What is entrepreneurship?
2. Explain the functions of an entrepreneur.

Chapter: 16

Money

Before we study monetary policy, we shall study about the definition and functions of money. Money has become so important that the modern economy is described as money economy. Modern economy cannot work without money. Even in the early stages of development, the need for exchange arose. But exchange took place first in the form of barter. Barter is the direct exchange of goods for goods. It is a system of trading without the use of money. In the past when wants of men were a few and simple, the barter system worked well. But as days passed by, it was found to be unsuitable. It had many difficulties. For example, barter requires double coincidence of wants. That is, a person must have what the other person wants and vice versa. And this is not always possible. For instance, if a person who has a cow wants a horse in exchange, the other person must have it and he must need a cow. Otherwise exchange cannot take place. Again, there is the difficulty of storage. Money serves as a store of value. In the absence of money, a person has to store his wealth in the form of commodities and they cannot be stored for a long period. For some commodities are perishables and some will lose their value?

16.1 Money

Money can be thought of as any good that is widely used or accepted in the transfer of goods and services. Today, there are three common forms of money in use. Commodity money is a good whose inherent value serves as the value of money – gold or silver being one good example. Fiat money is a good whose value is less than the value of money it represents – paper money, for instance. Bank money consists of accounting credits that can be drawn on by the depositor

16.2 Types of Money

8) Reserve Money

Reserve Money (RM) may be considered as Government money. (In this context, the Reserve Bank of India (RBI) is also taken as Government). Reserve money is the cash held by the public and the banks. It is composed of

C = currency with the public in circulation

OD = other deposits of the public with the RBI (OD) (The public regard their deposits with the RBI as cash or money) and

CR = cash reserves of banks. Cash reserves are composed of two parts: - They are (1) cash reserves with banks themselves and (2) Bankers deposits with RBI.

Thus,

$$\text{Reserve Money (RM)} = C + OD + CR$$

We may note that the simple theory of money supply states that supply of money (M) is an increasing function of reserve money (RM). In other words, as Reserve Money changes, supply of money also changes. The Reserve money is also called high powered money on account of its great influence on money supply.

9) **Fiat Money:** Currency notes in circulation are normally referred to as fiat money. For example, one Rupee notes issued by the Government of India is Fiat money. The notes issued by the RBI are usually referred to as bank notes. They are in the nature of promissory notes.

10) Dear Money

When there is inflation in a country, the central bank tries to control it by following dear money policy. The term "Dear Money" refers to a phase or policy when interest rates are high.

✓ **Cheap Money** "Cheap Money" denotes a phase in which loans are available at low rates of interest or a policy which creates this situation. Cheap money policy is followed by a central bank during a period of depression to increase the supply of money so as to stimulate investment.

16.3 Value of money

By "Value of Money" we mean the purchasing power of money. The purchasing power of money depends upon the price level. A general rise in the price level indicates a fall in the value of money and a general fall in prices indicates a rise in the value of money.

16.4 Measurement of Money

"The Federal Reserve publishes weekly and monthly data on three money supply measures -- M1, M2, and M3 .The money supply measures reflect the different degrees of liquidity that different types of money have. The narrowest measure, M1, is restricted to the most liquid forms of money; it consists of currency in the hands of the public; travelers checks; demand deposits, and other deposits against which checks can be written. M2 includes M1, plus savings accounts, time deposits , and balances in retail money market mutual funds. M3 includes M2 plus large-denomination time deposits, balances in institutional money funds, repurchase liabilities issued by depository institutions, and Eurodollars held by U.S. residents at foreign branches of U.S. banks and at all banks in the United Kingdom and Canada."

16.5 Functions of Money

Money has overcome the difficulties of barter. Crowther, has defined money as "anything that is generally acceptable as a means of exchange (i.e., as a means of settling debts) and that at the same time acts as a measure and as a store of value". An important point about this definition is that it regards anything that is generally acceptable as money. Thus money includes coins, currency notes, cheques, bills of exchange, credit cards and so on. That is why prof. Walker has said: "money is that which money does". By this, he has referred to the functions of money. Money performs many functions

152

in a modern economy. The most important functions of money are given in the form of a couplet quoted below:-

"Money is a matter of functions four A medium, a measure, a standard, a store". Thus, money, is a medium of exchange, a measure of value, a store of value and a standard of deferred payments.

- ✓ **Medium of exchange :**

  The most important function of money is that it acts as medium of exchange. Money is accepted freely in exchange for all other goods. Barter system is very inconvenient. So the introduction of money has got over the difficulty of barter.

- ✓ **Measure of value :**

  Money acts as a common measure of value. It is a unit of account and a standard of measurement. Whenever we buy a good in the market we pay a price for it in money. And price is nothing but value expressed in terms of money. So we can measure the value of a good by the money we pay for it. Just as we use yards and meters for measuring length and kilograms for measuring weights, we use money for measuring the value of goods. It makes economic calculations easy.

- ✓ **Store of value :**

  A man who wants to store his wealth in some convenient form will find money admirably suitable for the purpose. It acts as a store of value. Suppose the wealth of a man consists of a thousand cattle. It is rather difficult for him to preserve his wealth in the form of cattle. But if there is money, he can sell his cattle, get money for that and can store his wealth in the form of money.

✓ **Standard of deferred payments :**

Money is used as a standard for future (deferred) payments. It forms the basis for credit transactions. Business in modern times is based on credit to a large extent. This is facilitated by the existence of money. In credit, since payment is made at a future date, there must be some medium which will have as far as possible the same exchange power in the future as at present. If credit transactions were to be carried on the basis of commodities, there would be a lot of difficulties and it will affect trade. Money, to be used as a medium of exchange, must be universally acceptable. All people must accept a thing as money. Or, the Government should give it legal sanction. And for performing the other two functions, that is, to be used as a store of value and standard of deferred payments, money should have stability of value. In other words, the value of money should not change often.

16.6 Importance of Money

Money is one of the most fundamental inventions of mankind "Every branch of knowledge has its fundamental discovery. In mechanics, it is the wheel, in science fire, in politics the vote. Similarly in economics, in the whole commercial side of Man's social existence, money is the essential invention on which all the rest is based (Crowther). Money is indispensable in an economy

154

whether it is capitalistic or socialistic. Price mechanism plays a vital role in capitalism. Production, distribution and consumption are influenced to a great extent by prices, and prices are measured in money. Even a socialist economy, where the price system does not play so important a role as under capitalism, cannot do without money. For a while, the socialists talked of ending the money, i.e., abolishing money itself, because they considered money as an invention of the capitalists to suppress the working class. But later on they found that even under a system of planning, economic accounting would be impossible without the help of money.

In the early stages of civilization, different people used different things as money. Cattle, tobacco, shells, wheat, tea, salt, knives, leather, animals such as sheep, horses and oxen and metals like iron, lead, tin and copper have been used as money. Gradually precious metals such as gold and silver replaced other metals such as iron, copper and bronze as money. And now paper is used as money. We may describe one more form of money, that is, bank deposits which go from person to person by means of cheques.

16.7 Money supply

The Reserve Bank of India (RBI) is the central bank of India. It manages the monetary system of India. It has classified the money supply of our country into four components. They are as follows:

M1 = Currency with the public. It includes coins and currency notes + demand deposits of the public. M1 is also known as narrow money;

M2 = M1 + post office savings deposits;

M3 = M1 + Time deposits of the public with the banks. M3 is also known as broad money; and

M4 = M3 + total post office deposits.

Review of Questions

1. What is Money?
2. Define Fiat Money?
3. **Define Dear Money.**
4. Explain the functions of Money.

Chapter: 17

Monetary Policy

17.1 Monetary Policy

The basic goals of macroeconomic policy in most of the countries are full employment, price stability, rapid economic growth, balance of payments equilibrium and economic justice. Economic justice refers to equitable distribution of income. The government tries to achieve the

goals through macroeconomic policy. Macroeconomic policy can be broadly divided into monetary policy and fiscal policy. Of course, the government follows other policies such as industrial policy, agricultural policy, tariff policy and so on. But we limit our discussion only to monetary policy and the fiscal policy. In the present chapter, we shall study the monetary policy with reference to our country. "Monetary policy is policy that employs the central bank's control over the supply and cost of money as an instrument for achieving the objectives of economic policy" (Edward Shapiro).

17.2 Instruments of Monetary Policy

Roughly we may say that monetary policy is credit control policy. The instruments of credit control can be broadly divided into:

- ✓ Quantitative credit control measures; and
- ✓ Selective credit control measures.

17.2.1 Quantitative credit control

Quantitative credit control instruments include bank rate policy, variation of cash reserve ratios and open market operations.

- ✓ **Bank Rate:** The Bank rate is the minimum rate at which the central bank of a country will lend money to all other banks. Suppose, there is too much of money in circulation. Then the central bank should take some money out of circulation. It can do it by increasing the bank rate. When the bank rate goes up, the rates charged by other banks go up. The belief is that if the rate of interest goes up, businessmen will be discouraged to borrow more money and producers will borrow less money for investment. Generally, to control inflation, the central bank will increase the bank rate.

- ✓ **Cash Reserve Ratios:** The ability of a commercial bank to create credit depends upon its cash reserves. The central bank of a country has the power to vary the cash reserve ratios. During inflation, to check the sharp rise in commodity prices and to control credit, the central bank can make use of this weapon.

- ✓ **Open Market Operations:** In India, the open market operations have been conducted in Central Government securities and State Government securities. The success of open market operations as a weapon of credit control, depends mainly on (i) the possession by the central bank of adequate volume of securities ; (2) the presence of well developed bill (securities) market ; and (3) stability of cash reserve ratios maintained by commercial banks. These things are missing to a great degree in India. So, open market operations have not become a powerful weapon of credit control in our country. They have been largely used in India more to assist the Government in its borrowing operations rather than controlling credit.

17.2.2 Selective credit controls

Selective credit controls can play an important role in an underdeveloped money market with a planned economy. Unlike the instruments of quantitative credit control, the selective instruments affect the types of credit extended by commercial banks. They not only prevent flow of credit into undesirable channels, but also direct the flow of credit into useful channels. The Reserve Bank of India had started applying the selective credit controls since 1955. The weapons of selective credit controls include

- ✓ Fixing minimum margin of lending or for purchase of securities. (For example, shares or commodities like food grains and raw materials which are in short supply). In this case, the central bank specifies the fraction of the purchase price of securities that must be paid in cash. Unlike general controls, selective controls make it possible for the central

159

bank to restrain what is regarded as an unhealthy expansion of credit. (eg. for financing the purchase of securities or automobiles)

✓ Ceiling on the amount of credit for expansion and

✓ Different rates of interest will be charged to encourage certain sectors and to discourage certain other sectors. In our country, the last weapon has been used especially, to encourage exports, agricultural production and production in small scale and cottage industries sector.

✓ The central bank will persuade the commercial banks to follow certain policies through moral suasion.

Review of Questions

1. What is Monetary Policy?
2. Define Bank Rate.
3. Define Open Market Operation.
4. Explain the instruments of Monetary Policy.

Chapter: 18

Inflation

18.1 Meaning of Inflation:

Inflation is a key concept in macroeconomics, and a major concern for government policymakers, companies, workers and investors. Inflation refers to a broad increase in prices across many goods and services in an economy over a sustained period of time. Conversely, inflation can also be thought of as the erosion in value of an economy's currency (a unit of currency buys fewer goods and services than in prior periods).

18.2   Measurement of Inflation:

Tools of measurement of Inflation are as follows:

✓ **Consumer Price Index:**

In the United States, the Consumer Price Index (CPI) is among the most commonly-used measures of inflation. The CPI uses a so-called "market basket" of goods to measure the changes in prices experienced by average consumers in the

161

economy. Economists and central bankers will often subdivide the CPI into so-called "core inflation," a measure that excludes the price of food and energy.

- ✓ **The Producer Price Index:**

The Producer Price Index (PPI) is a measure of inflation that tracks the prices that producers obtain for their goods. Though a long-followed economic statistic, the change in composition of some economies away from manufacturing and towards services is eroding the value of this statistic.

- ✓ **The GDP Deflator:**

The GDP deflator is another option for measuring prices and inflation. As the name suggests, the GDP deflator is a price measurement tool that is used to convert nominal GDP to real GDP. The GDP deflator is a broader measure than the CPI, as it includes goods and services bought by businesses and governments. While there is little consensus on the "right" rate of inflation for an economy (or even if inflation is necessary at all), there is little disagreement in the differing impacts of expected and unexpected inflation.

18.3 Inflation and Deflation

The terms 'inflation' and 'deflation' are not easy to define. Different economists have defined them in different ways. Crowther has given us the most simple and useful definition of these terms. According to Crowther, "Inflation is a state in which the value of money is falling, i.e., prices are rising". So it is generally regarded that during a period of inflation, the price level will rise. It is also described as a situation where too much money chases too few goods resulting in an abnormal increase of price level. Shapiro has defined inflation as "a persistent and appreciable rise in the general level of prices". And Harry Johnson has defined it as a "sustained rise in prices". However, we should remember one important point. That is, there can be inflation even without a rise in the price level. This is known as *'Repressed Inflation'*. Usually this happens during a war period. On account of many controls and rationing that exist during wartime, prices will be kept under check. But the moment controls are withdrawn, prices will go up. So the real test of inflation is neither an increase in the amount of money nor a rise in prices, but the appearance of abnormal profits. Whenever businessmen and producers make huge profits, it is a sign of inflation. But inflation is not positive for all type of professionals. Some people lose money in Inflation.

18.3   Types of Inflation

Various types of Inflation is given below:

18.4.1 Demand – Pull Inflation

It is loosely described as "too much money chasing too few goods". This refers to the situation where general price level rises because the demand for goods and services exceeds the supply available at the existing prices.

- ✓ **Creeping or Persistent inflation:** Since the end of world War II, i.e. since 1945, there has been a tendency for prices and wages to push one another upwards. This situation has been described as creeping or persistent inflation.

- ✓ **Runaway or Galloping or Hyper – Inflation:** This is a serious type of inflation. For example, it was experienced in Germany after World War I and in Hungary and China after World War II. In this situation, prices rise to a very great extent at high speed and high prices have to be paid even for cheap things. And money becomes quite worthless and new currency has to be introduced. This situation is known as galloping inflation or hyper-inflation.

18.4.2 Cost – Push Inflation

Cost – push inflation is induced by rising costs, including wages, so that rising wages and other costs push up prices. We can also speak of wage inflation or price inflation when we mean increase in wages or prices.

- ✓ **Bottleneck Inflation:** This refers to inflation that results from shortages, imbalances and rising marginal costs as full employment output is approached.

- ✓ **Profit – Push Inflation:-** Just as trade unions manage to push up wages, oligopolists and monopolists will raise prices more than enough to cover increase in costs with the aim of making monopoly profits. Generally during war and in the post- war period, there will be inflation. This is so because during war, the incomes of people increase. But there will be shortage of goods and there may be rationing, control and things like that. So during the post - war years, people who have been forced to save money will spend. That is, demand for all sorts of goods will increase during that period but

164

supply will not increase so fast as that. This leads to inflation. Inflation occurs during war because the one great aim at that time is that of winning the war. Since modern wars are so expensive, the Government has to depend upon created money to finance war. This leads to inflation. And inflation breeds inflation. It means that inflation leads to inflation. During a period of inflation, prices will be high. Since prices are high, workers will demand high wages. High wages result in high costs. High costs in turn lead to high prices. Thus it forms a vicious circle. "Wages force up prices ; prices force up wages". This is the *inflationary spiral*. "Deficit financing" is another cause of inflation. This applies particularly to underdeveloped countries with planned economies. Inflationary trends can be noticed also during the boom period of a trade cycle.

Since inflation has many evils, every government tries to check it. Inflation has destroyed many economies. For example the inflation that took place in 1923 in Germany destroyed her economic system. Inflation can be checked by some or all of the following measures. (1) Increased taxation (2) By reducing government expenditure on capital projects. (In India, this measure has been suggested to check inflation. Many capital projects proposed in our Third Five

Year Plan were either suspended or dropped completely. (3) Restrictions on imports. (4)Rationing and (5) Price controls. Sometimes a "wage freeze' is recommended to check inflation. That is, trade unions will be requested not to ask for an increase in wages during a given period. The success of the above measures in tackling inflation depends upon the efficiency of the government in implementing the measures.

18.5 Effects of Inflation:

Changes in prices affect different sections of the community in different ways. They affect production and distribution too.

✓ **Effects on production**

If prices are rising, it will stimulate production. Under a capitalistic system, production is carried on mainly for profits. During a period of rising prices (inflation), there will be abnormal profits. This increases production. So manufacturers and businessmen gain during inflation. Producers and businessmen gain during inflation. Producers gain by inflation because during that period prices rise faster than costs. So they make huge profits. But if inflation becomes hyper-inflation, it may end in a crash. On account of the rapid fall in the value of money, profits which are in the form of money may become worthless. And there will be a "flight from currency". Inflation may become an important cause of "violent revolutions and economic chaos". In a period of falling prices, businessmen incur huge losses because prices fall faster than costs. And there will be little scope for investment. This results in unemployment on large scale. There will be business depression. During depression, money may be cheaply available, prices of materials will be low, men will be available for work but there will be no investment, no employment, no incomes and no demand for goods. Such a situation has been described as 'poverty in the midst of plenty.' The Great Depression of 1930s is a case in point.

✓ **Effects on Distribution**

a) **Business class:** During inflation, manufacturers and businessmen make huge profits. Of course, during deflation, they make losses.

b) **Fixed income groups:** People in fixed income groups are hit hard in times of inflation. The incomes of wage earners and salaried people such as teachers, clerks and judges do not increase as fast as prices. Even retired people getting pension are also affected during inflation. Wage earners and salaried – people gain during a period of falling prices. But it is not a real gain because many people will lose their jobs during deflation. Unemployment is a worse evil than rising prices.

c) **Investors:** people who have invested their money in "gilt edged" securities (government securities) will get only fixed income. So their position is like those in the fixed income group. But those who have shares in companies will make profits during a period of rising prices and lose during a period of falling prices. In Germany, thousands of middle class families were ruined during the inflation because all their lifetime savings were reduced to nothing by the tremendous rise in prices. If the value of money falls continuously, it becomes unsuitable as a store of value. People will not save at all.

d) **Debtor:** Debtor gain during deflation and lose during inflation. But the gain during deflation is only a temporary feature. It can be seen from the above discussion that violent changes in prices are a bad thing. Both inflation and deflation are great evils. *"Inflation is unjust and deflation is inexpedient"* (disadvantageous). Some economists believe that of the two, deflation is worse because it results in unemployment. That is why it is now generally agreed that a steadily rising price level is a good thing for economic progress and social justice. We may agree with Robertson when he says that "money which is a source of so many blessings to mankind becomes also, unless we can control it, a source of peril and confusion".

Review of Questions

1. What is Inflation?
2. Define Demand pull Inflation?
3. Define Cost push Inflation.
4. Explain the effects of Inflation.
5. Describe the different types of Inflation.

Chapter: 19

Business Cycle

19.1 Meaning of Business Cycle:

The business cycle is the pattern of expansion, contraction and recovery in the economy. Generally speaking, the business cycle is measured and tracked in terms of GDP and unemployment – GDP rises and unemployment shrinks during expansion phases, while reversing in periods of recession. Wherever one starts in the cycle, the economy is observed to go through four periods – expansion, peak, contraction and trough. Parkin and Bade's text *Economics* gives the following definition of the business cycle: "The **business cycle** is the periodic but irregular up-and-down movements in economic activity, measured by fluctuations in real GDP and other macroeconomic variables." To put it simply, the business cycle is defined as the real fluctuations in economic activity and gross domestic product (GDP) over a period of time. The fact that the economy experiences these ups-and-downs in activity should be no surprise. In fact, all modern industrial economies like that of the United States endure considerable swings in economic activity over time. The ups may be marked by indicators like high growth and low unemployment while the downs are generally defined by low or stagnant growth and high unemployment. Given its relationship to the phases of the business cycle, unemployment is but one of the various economic indicators used to measure economic activity. For most detailed information about how various economic indicators and their relationship to the business cycle, check out A Beginner's Guide to Economic Indicators. Parkin and Bade go on to explain that despite the name, the business cycle is not a regular, predictable, or repeating cycle. Though its phases can be defined, its timing is random and, to a large degree, unpredictable.

19.2 The Phases of the Business Cycle

While no two business cycles are exactly the same, they can be identified as a sequence of four phases that were classified and studied in their most modern sense by American economists Arthur Burns and Wesley Mitchell in their text *Measuring Business Cycles*. The four primary phases of the business cycle include:

- ✓ **Expansion:** A speedup in the pace of economic activity defined by high growth, low unemployment, and increasing prices. The period marked from trough to peak.
- ✓ **Peak:** The upper turning point of a business cycle and the point at which expansion turns into contraction.

- ✓ **Contraction:** A slowdown in the pace of economic activity defined by low or stagnant growth, high unemployment, and declining prices. It is the period from peak to trough.
- ✓ **Trough:** The lowest turning point of a business cycle in which a contraction turns into an expansion. This turning point is also called
- ✓ **Recovery**: After reaching lowest point of a business cycle, economic activities again increase. This is a positive phase.

These four phases also make up what is known as the "boom-and-bust" cycles, which are characterized as business cycles in which the periods of expansion are swift and the subsequent contraction is steep and severe.

19.3 Recessions

A recession occurs if a contraction is severe enough. The National Bureau of Economic Research (NBER) identifies a recession as a contraction or significant decline in economic activity "lasting more than a few months, normally visible in real GDP, real income, employment, industrial production." Along the same vein, a deep trough is called a slump or a depression. The difference between a recession and a depression, which is not well-understood by non-economists, is explained in this helpful guide: Recession is typically used to mean a downturn in economic activity, but most economists use a specific definition of "two consecutive quarters of declining real GDP" for recession. By comparison, there is no formal definition of depression. While recessions have averaged around 10 months in length since the 1950s, the recovery/expansion phases have a much wider range of lengths, though around three years is relatively common. The movement of the economy through business cycles also highlights certain economic relationships. While growth will rise and fall with cycles, there is a long-term trend line for growth; when economic growth is above the trend line, unemployment usually falls. One expression of this relationship is Okun's Law, an equation that holds that every 1% of GDP above trend equates to 0.5% less unemployment. The relationship between inflation and growth is not as clear, but inflation does tend to fall during recessions and then increase through recoveries. While the business cycle is a relatively simple concept, there is great debate among economists as to what influences the length and magnitude of the individual parts of the cycle, and whether the government can (or should) play a role in influencing this process. Keynesians, for instance, believe that the government can soften the impact of recessions (and shorten their duration) by cutting taxes and increasing spending, while also preventing an economy from "overheating" by increasing taxes and cutting spending during expansion phases.

In comparison, many monetarist economists disagree with the notion of business cycles altogether and prefer to look at changes in the economy as irregular (non-cyclical) fluctuations. In many cases, they believe that declines in business activity are the result of monetary phenomena and that active government inflation is ineffective at best and destabilizing at worst.

There are numerous other alternate theories on the business cycle and its causes/influences. Real business cycle theorists, for instance, believe that it is external shocks like innovation and technological progress that drive cycles, and that issues like excessive overcapacity can drive downturns. Other theorists suggest that excess speculation or the creation of excess levels of bank drive business cycles.

Review of Questions

1. What is Business Cycle?
2. Define Recessions?
3. Explain the different phases of Inflation.

Chapter: 20

Employment and Unemployment

According to Stephen Simpson, Labor is a driving force in every economy – wages paid for labor fuel consumer spending, and the output of labor is essential for companies. Likewise, unemployed workers represent wasted potential production within an economy. Consequently, unemployment is a significant concern within macroeconomics. In Economics, unemployment refers to the number of civilian workers who are actively looking for work and not currently receiving wages. Given that official unemployment statistics specifically exclude those who would like to work but have become discouraged and ceased looking for employment, the true unemployment rate is always higher than the official rate.

20.1 Types of Unemployment:

✓ **Frictional Unemployment:** Frictional unemployment results from imperfect information and the difficulties in matching qualified workers with jobs. A college graduate who is actively looking for work is one example. Frictional unemployment is almost impossible to avoid, as neither job-seekers nor employers can have perfect information or act instantaneously, and it is generally not seen as problematic to an economy.

✓ **Cyclical Unemployment:** Cyclical unemployment refers to unemployment that is a product of the business cycle. During recessions, for instance, there is often inadequate demand for labor and wages are typically slow to fall to a point where the demand and supply of labor are back in balance.

✓ **Structural Unemployment:** Structural employment refers to unemployment that occurs when workers are not qualified for the jobs that are available. Workers in this case are often out of work for much longer periods of time and often require retraining. Structural unemployment can be a serious problem within an economy, particularly in cases where entire sectors (manufacturing, for instance) become obsolete.

While high unemployment is undesirable, full employment (meaning zero unemployment) is neither practical nor desirable. When economists talk about full employment, frictional unemployment and some small percentage of structural unemployment are excluded. Economists do not generally believe it is practical or desirable to have 100% employment in an economy.

In particular, the Phillips curve highlights why this is so. Generally there is a relationship between inflation and unemployment – the lower the rate of unemployment, the higher the rate of inflation.

While a variety of factors can alter the curve (including productivity gains), the essential take-away is that neither a zero-unemployment or zero-inflation scenario is viable on a long-term basis. There is also a tradeoff between employment and efficiency. Businesses maximize their profits when they produce the largest number of goods possible at the lowest price possible. In some cases, though, labour is more expensive (less efficient) than capital equipment. Consequently, there is always a trade-off between the cost and productivity of labour and that of labour-substituting capital equipment and that effectively reduces the number of jobs available. Likewise, structural employment is a recurrent problem as technology progresses – workers find their skills no longer match the needs of the employers and must update their training as industries adopt new technologies.

Review of Questions

1. What is Unemployment?
2. Explain the types of Unemployment.

Chapter: 21

International trade

21.1 Meaning of International Trade

International trade is the exchange of goods, services and capital across national borders. It is a multi-trillion dollar activity, central to the GDP of many countries, and it is the only way for people in many countries to acquire resources they require. Absent trade, consumers and suppliers are forced to either develop substitute goods or devote a large percentage of their income to acquiring products where demand is inelastic and domestic supply is inadequate. Two of the key concepts in the economics of international trade are specialization and comparative advantage.

21.2 Absolute Advantage:

It seems readily apparent that countries can benefit from trade if each country does something better than the other (i.e. can produce goods or services at a lower cost). What if one company is more efficient in *every* good? This situation is called absolute advantage.

21.3 Comparative Advantage:

Even in situations of absolute advantage, though, there can be benefits to trade. As long as a country is not equally superior in producing all goods, there will be different relative costs for producing various goods. This is where comparative advantage comes in; so long as the two countries have different relative efficiencies, the two countries can benefit from trade – the country with absolute advantage will still benefit by directing its resources to those goods where it is most productive and trading for the others.

21.4 Specialization:

Specialization refers to this process; countries (as well as individual businesses) can maximize their welfare by specializing in the production of those goods where they are most efficient and enjoy the largest advantages over rivals.

21.5 Balance Of Payments:

A country's balance of payments basically tracks the financial flows between trading partners. The balance of payments includes the payments made for imports and exports, as well as financial transfers. Exports create a positive entry, while imports are a negative. That said, a balance of payments must always balance out at zero – a trade deficit (more imports than exports) must be balanced with foreign investments, declines in reserves, or increased debt; likewise, a trade surplus will be balanced out with financial outflows or increased reserves.

21.6 Current Account:

Within a nation's balance of payment is the current account. The current account is made up primary of a company's trade balance (exports minus imports), as well as net interest and dividends, and net transfer payments

21.7 Impediments to Trade

While free trade is generally thought of as a positive, countries will periodically put up barriers to trade. Tariffs are taxes on imports that make imported goods more expensive and less competitive relative to domestically-produced goods. While national governments used to obtain a significant percentage of their receipts from tariffs (in the days before income taxes were common), tariffs today are more commonly used to protect domestic industries and/or to punish other countries for perceived wrongdoing (typically subsidizing local industries to the detriment of the importing country's industries).

✓ **Subsidies**:

Subsidies are transfer payments given by governments to domestic suppliers of goods or services. The motivation to provide subsidies is to increase production and/or lower prices for a country's consumers and/or to make domestically-produced goods more competitive with imports.

✓ **Quotas**:

Quotas are limits on the amount of a good that can be imported in a given period. Quotas serve a similar purpose to tariffs in that the increase the price of imported goods, but

179

quotas can be even more severe as no additional goods are available once the quota level is reached.

Review of Questions

1. What is International Trade?
2. Define Absolute Advantage.
3. Define Comparative Advantage.

Chapter: 22

Exchange Rate

22.1 Meaning of Exchange Rate

For citizens of different countries to conduct trade, they have to buy and sell each other's currencies. The price of a nation's currency, expressed as an amount of a second country's currency, is referred to as the exchange rate. As exchange rates play a significant role in trade and capital flows, it is an important concept in macroeconomics. The nominal exchange rate is the type of exchange rate that is referenced most often in business discussions. When reports talk of the dollar being worth 1.35 Euros or 85 Japanese yen, they are referring to the nominal exchange rate. The real exchange rate is a bit more academic – it is the amount of goods or services from one country that can be traded for another country's goods and services. It can be expressed as the equation: (nominal exchange rate x domestic price) / foreign price.

22.2 Types of Exchange Rate

There are basically two types of international exchange rate systems – fixed and floating.

- ✓ **Fixed Exchange Rate**: In a fixed exchange system, countries establish the ratio of their currencies and then commit to maintaining those rates. A country supports fixed rates by buying or selling foreign reserves in response to changes in demand for the currency. From day to day, there is minimal change in a fixed rate system – if the exchange rate between Dollars and Euros is fixed at 1:1.25, businesses, governments and individuals can typically count on that rate being in force at any given time. This is often seen as convenient for companies conducting international trade as it removes the risk and unpredictability of exchange rates. Fixed rates were commonplace throughout the 19th and 20th centuries, with gold serving as the underlying standard and the British pound serving as the global reserve currency (in other words, almost all countries would accept gold or British pounds to settle accounts). Near the end of World War 2nd, the Bretton Woods Agreement came into being and largely governed foreign exchange rates into the early 1970s, with fixed rates and the U.S. dollar becoming the new world reserve currency. In practice, most countries have found that a fixed exchange system is too limiting and too expensive to maintain, and as of the early part of the 21st century, China is the only major economy to maintain such a system.

✓ **Floating Exchange Rate:** In contrast, a country can elect to allow the market to set the value of its currency. This is called a floating exchange rate system. If a country has floating exchange rates, foreign exchange rates are subject to the same rules of supply and demand as any other good. When there is increased demand for a currency, its value increases relative to other currencies. This demand can be driven by consumer tastes (a preference for goods from that country), relative incomes, relative inflation and outright speculation. Not surprisingly, exchange rates are typically much more volatile in a floating environment; some economists have estimated that rates have been at least twice as volatile since the end of the Bretton Woods system.

22.3   Determinants of Exchange Rates

One theory, called purchasing power parity (PPP), holds that the ratio of two countries' exchange rates should equal the ratio of the prices of identical goods in those two countries. If a gold coin is worth $1 in the United States and the same gold coin would be worth 100 yen in Japan, PPP says that the exchange rate should be $1:100Y. By extension, then, purchasing power parity also holds that changes in relative inflation rates tie into changes in exchange rates. This theory works mathematically and logically; if there was not such a state of parity, one could buy goods in the "cheap" country, sell them in the more expensive country and reap risk-free profits. In the real world, though, this theory does not strictly hold true. Not only are there expenses involved in shipping, but there are various trade barriers and tax issues involved. What's more, the notions of specialization and comparative advantage suggest that goods are not exactly the same – some countries can produce goods at lower cost than other countries. Still, when considering price levels on the whole this is less problematic and the theory is somewhat more useful. One well-known application of purchasing power theory is the Big Mac Index. Created by The Economist, the Big Mac Index evaluates the under/overvaluation of foreign currency relative to current rates by examining the price of a Big Mac in various countries. In concept this should be a reasonably fair test of purchasing power theory, though local taxes, regulations and farm policy to influence the comparisons.

Likewise, the interest rate parity concept is a useful theoretical construct that does not hold true in practice. In essence, interest rate parity holds that the returns from borrowing money in one currency (say dollars), exchanging it for another (yen), investing that currency in interest-earning assets denominated in that second currency (yen-denominated bonds), and purchasing a futures contract to convert back to dollars at maturity of the asset (the bonds) will be equal to simply buying and holding like interest-bearing assets in the original currency (a dollar-denominated bond in this case).

This concept implies that the differences in nominal interest rates correspond to the difference in rates of change of exchange rates. Now it is certainly true that there is a relationship between interest rates and foreign currency exchange rates. There is a

184

phenomenon in international investing called "yield shopping" where investors seek out interest rates that seem to be in excess of what the exchange rates would indicate. Along these lines, an overvalued currency is associated with relatively low expected inflation and high expected real interest rates. Still, actual experience deviates from this model due at least in part to the fact that there are costs and taxes involved in these transactions and other factors can influence rates as well. Interestingly, actual experience with real floating exchange rates has shown much less connection between real exchange rates and rates of growth in inflation and monetary supplies. In practice, fluctuations in real exchange rates reflect market forces and investor expectations.

Relative interest rates play a major role in exchange rates between countries. Higher rates will often have the effect of attracting capital to that country, increasing the demand for the currency and lifting the exchange rate.

Review of Questions

1. What is Exchange Rate?
2. Explain the types of Exchange Rate.
3. Describe the determinants of Exchange Rate.

Chapter: 23

Budgeting

23.1 Budget

Meaning: Government's revenue and expenditure decisions are presented in the budget. Budget, being an essential and important element of planning and development, provide the specific development objectives to be pursued and the required policy direction. They are necessary because income and expenditure do not occur simultaneously. Thus, 'budget' has been defined as the annual financial statement of the estimated receipts and proposed expenditure of the government in a financial year, usually April 1 to March 31 of the next year. The term budget is derived from the French word 'Bougette'. It means 'small bag'. As such, the Finance minister of a country carries a bag containing abstracts of budget papers while presenting the budget in the Parliament or a State Legislature. The governments, both Union and State, prepare their budget every financial year. Government budget indicates the probable income and expenditure of the government, the financial policies, taxation measures, investment opportunities, extent of saving, utilization of resources, mobilization of capital etc.

23.2 Definition

Various definitions have been formulated for the concept of Budget. Prof. Dimock says, "A budget is a balanced estimate of expenditures and receipts for a given period of time. In the hands of the administration, the budget is record of past performance, a method of current control and a projection of future plans". To quote Gladstone, "Budgets are not merely matters of arithmetic but in a thousand ways go to the root of prosperity of individuals and relation of classes and the strength of Kingdom". Therefore, the budget is a document containing preliminary approval plan of public revenue and expenditures. It bridges the proposed revenue and proposed expenditure for the budget period.

23.3 Kinds of Budget

✓ **Balanced Budget:** A balanced budget is that, over a period of time, revenue does not fall short of expenditure. In other words government budget is said to be balanced when its tax revenue and expenditure are equal.

✓ **Unbalanced Budget (Surplus or deficit):** An unbalanced budget is that, over a period of time, revenue exceeds expenditure or expenditure exceeds revenue. In other words, the government's income or tax revenue and expenditure are not equal. When there is an excess of income over expenditure, it is called a surplus budget. On the other hand, when there is an excess of expenditure over income, it is a case of deficit budget. Classical economists advocated balanced budget. But it is not always helpful in achieving and sustaining economic growth. Modern economists argue that an unbalanced budget is very useful for achieving and maintaining economic stability.

✓ **Revenue Budget and Capital Budget:** Budgeting is the most important constituent of the financial administration. Preparation of the budget is one of the main operations of budgeting. It is mandatory for the government to make a statement of estimated receipts and expenditures which must be laid before the Parliament every financial year. It has to distinguish expenditure on revenue account and capital account from other expenditures. So government budget comprises Revenue Budget and Capital Budget.

✓ **Revenue Budget:** Revenue budget consists of revenue receipts of the government (tax revenue and non-tax revenue) and the expenditure met from these revenues. Expenditures which do not result in creation of assets are called revenue expenditure. (e.g. current revenues and current expenditure for normal functioning of the Government departments, interest charges on debt incurred by Govt. and other no developmental expenditure).

✓ **Capital Budget:** Majority of the government expenditures form the capital expenditure. Capital budget consists of receipts and payments. Capital receipts are loans raised by government from the public which are called market loans, borrowings from the RBI, sale of treasury bills, loans received from foreign governments etc. Capital payments are expenditure on assets creation such as land, buildings, machinery, equipment investment loans to government companies and state governments and other developmental expenditures.

✓ **Performance Budgeting:** The process of fund allocation of governments in various countries has been changed from traditional expenditure budgeting to new forms of rationalistic budgeting, such as performance budgeting, programme budgeting and zero based budgeting. Under performance budgeting, various activities of the government are identified in the budget both in financial and physical terms. This is necessary to ascertain the relationship between input and output and to assess the performance in relation to cost. Performance budgeting is conceived as a system of presenting public expenditure in terms of distinguishable divisions such as government functions, programmes, activities and projects; such presentation would reflect the cost of running the government. Under this technique, funds are granted for carrying out specific amount of work identified under a particular division. A cost-benefit approach is employed which facilitates meaningful and purposeful allocation of funds. This method of budget technique promotes cost consciousness as well as cost efficiency and suggests corrections wherever required in the process of allocation of funds.

✓ **Zero based Budgeting:** Traditional technique of budgeting have been found to be inadequate for the reason that, the previous year's cost level is taken as the base for current year's budget. The traditional methods have not completely addressed the problem of efficiency in the matter of allocation of funds for various divisions. There is therefore a need for a new technique of budgeting which devices and uses a meaningful base for budgeting. Zero Based Budgeting is one such technique of budgeting. In zero based budgeting, every year is considered as a new year thus providing a connecting link between the previous year and the current year. The past performance and programmes are not taken into account. The budget is viewed as entirely a fresh and whole fiscal initiative i.e. from zero bases. Zero based budgeting evaluates and prioritizes the programmes of action at different levels. Each department has to justify its budget from its perspectives; evaluating feasible alternatives, before final selection and execution, the funds will be allocated for the selected programmes.

Review of Questions

1. What is Budget?
2. Explain the kinds of Budget.

Chapter: 24

Public Expenditure, Revenue, Debt and Taxes

24.1   Public Expenditure

Since the modern government represents a welfare state, the responsibility of the government is to bring about maximum social welfare. In addition to this, it has to perform various other functions, which require heavy expenditures. We study in this sub-division, the fundamental principles governing the flow of government funds into different spending streams and the methods of incurring expenditure on the various activities.

24.2   Public Revenue

Public revenue means different sources of government's income. It deals with the methods of raising revenue for the government, principles of taxation and other related problems. Raising of tax revenue and nontax revenue is the subject matter of public revenue. Tax revenue deals with the kinds of taxes and the impact and incidence of various taxes. Non-tax revenue includes

- ✓ Commercial revenue (income earned through sale of goods and services and profits earned by public sector enterprises),
- ✓ Administrative revenues (Fees, license fees, special assessments),
- ✓ Gifts and grants.

24.3   Public debt

The problem relating to the raising and repayment of public loans is studied under this sub-division. Borrowing by the government from the public is called public debt. In modern world, it is not possible for the government to meet all its expenditure through tax and non-tax revenue. Hence public revenue falls short of public expenditure. As a result, governments are forced to borrow from internal and external sources. In the case of internal debt, Government borrows from the people, commercial banks and the central bank. External debt includes borrowing from international monetary institutions like IMF and World Bank and also from foreign countries. The soundness of the borrowing policy of the governments and indication of the healthy direction of spending are examined under this sub-division.

24.4   Financial administration

Financial administration is concerned with the organization and functioning of the government machinery that is responsible for performing various financial activities of the state. Preparing the budget for the particular financial year is the master financial plan of the government. The various works, starting with the objectives of designing a budget, the methods of preparing it, presentation of the budget before the Parliament and State Assembly, passing or sanctioning by the Parliament, execution, auditing, implementation etc., constitute the subject matter of financial administration.

24.5   Federal Finance

Federal finance is a part of the study of public finance. A federation is an association of two or more states. In a federal form of government, there are: Central, State, and local governments. The interrelationships between these forms of governments, and the problems related to them and the financial functions of all these units are studied under federal finance.

24.6 Meaning of Tax

A tax is one of the important sources of public revenue. A tax is a compulsory charge or payment levied by the government on an individual or corporation. Therefore an element of compulsion is involved in taxation. Other sources of public revenue are excluded from this compulsory element. There is no direct give and take relationship between a taxpayer and the government. According to Prof. Seligman, "A tax is a compulsory contribution from the person to the State to defray the expenditure incurred in the common interest of all without any reference to the special benefits conferred". In the words of Dalton, "A tax is a compulsory contribution imposed by the public authority, irrespective of the exact amount of service rendered to the taxpayer, in return for whom no specific and direct *quid pro quo* is rendered to the payer". From these definitions, it is clear that tax is a compulsory contribution. It means that the State has the right to tax. Refusal to pay the tax is punishable. The phrase 'without *quid pro quo*' means the absence of direct and proportional benefit to the taxpayer from the government.

24.7 Canons of Taxation

Canons of taxation are considered as fundamental principles of taxation. Adam Smith laid down the following canons of taxation:

a) Canon of equity

b) Canon of certainty

c) Canon of convenience

d) Canon of economy

✓ **Canon of equity**

This canon is also called the 'ability to pay' principle of taxation. It means that taxes should be imposed according to the capacity of the tax payer. Poor should be taxed less and rich should be taxed more. This canon involves the principle of justice. All persons contribute according to their ability. As the cost of running the government should be equally borne by all, this canon is justified.

✓ **Canon of certainty**

Every tax payer should know the amount of tax to be paid, when to be paid, and where to be paid and also should be certain about the rate of tax to make investment decisions..

✓ **Canon of convenience**

Tax payment should be convenient and less burdensome to the tax payer. e.g. income tax collected at source, sales tax collected at the time of sales and land tax collected after harvest.

✓ **Canon of economy**

This canon signifies that the cost of collecting the revenue should be kept at the minimum possible level. The tax laws and procedures should be made simple, so as to reduce the expenses in maintaining people's income tax accounts. i.e. administrative expenditure to be kept at a minimum.

24.8 Types of taxes

Taxes are of different types. They are:

1. Direct and Indirect taxes

According to Dalton, "A direct tax is one which is really paid by a person on whom it is imposed whereas an indirect tax, though imposed on a person, is partly or wholly paid by another". In the case of a direct tax, the tax payer who pays a direct tax is also the tax bearer. In the case of indirect taxes, the taxpayer and the tax bearer are different persons.

✓ **Direct taxes:** Direct taxes are collected from the public directly. That it is to say, these taxes are imposed on and collected from the same person. One cannot evade paying the tax if it is imposed on him. Income tax, wealth tax, corporate tax, gift tax, estate duty, expenditure tax are good examples of direct taxes.

✓ **Indirect taxes:** Taxes imposed on commodities and services are termed as indirect taxes. There is a chance for shifting the burden of indirect taxes. The incidence is upon the person who ultimately pays it. Examples of indirect taxes are excise duties, customs duties and sales taxes (commodity taxes). The classification of direct taxes and indirect taxes is based on the criterion of shifting of the incidence of tax. The burden of a direct tax is borne by the person on whom it is levied. For example, income tax is a direct tax. Its burden falls on the person who is liable to pay it to the government. He cannot transfer the burden to some other person. An indirect tax is initially paid by one person but ultimately the burden of the tax is fully or partially borne by another person. Because there is a possibility of transfer of burden of an indirect tax. For example, the excise duty on a motor-bike is initially paid by the manufacturer. But he subsequently shifts this burden to the consumer by including the tax in the price of the bike. Roughly, we may say that the direct taxes are paid by the rich and the indirect taxes are paid by the poor.

2. Progressive, Proportional, Regressive and Digressive taxes

Direct taxes can also be classified on the basis of the degree of progressiveness or distribution of their burden on the tax payers. Ability of the people to pay a tax is measured on the basis of property, income, size of the family and consumption etc. The ability to pay in practice implies tax base and tax rate. Tax base denotes the income, property and expenditure on the basis of which ability to pay the tax is measured. Rate structure indicates equalization of burden of taxation. Tax rate is the percentage of tax levied per unit

196

of tax base. The total amount of tax is equal to the tax base multiplied by tax rate.

- ✓ **Proportional tax:** In the case of a proportional tax, tax rate remains constant regardless of whether the tax base is large or small. It means uniform tax rate is imposed on the rich as well as the poor. The tax paid by the people is fixed in proportion to their income and wealth and other tax bases.

- ✓ **Progressive tax:** In the case a progressive tax, the tax rate increases as the tax base increases. With the increase in income, a taxpayer has to pay a higher tax. For example, in the case of income tax, exemption limit and tax slabs are characterized by the income tax structure formulated by the government of India. As each income slab increases, there is an increase in the rates of tax.

- ✓ **Regressive tax:** When the tax liability on income falls with the increase in the tax payer's income, it is termed as a regressive tax. Here, the tax rate decreases as the tax base increases. Under this tax system, the poorer sections of the society are taxed at higher rates than the richer sections and hence this tax is not just or equitable.

- ✓ **Digressive tax:** Digressive tax is a blend of progressive tax and proportional tax. The rate of taxation increases up to a point. After that limit, a uniform rate is charged. Here the rate of tax does not increase in the same proportion as the increase in income. Under this tax system, the higher income groups make less sacrifice than the lower income groups.

Review of Questions

1. What is Public Expenditure?
2. Define Public Debt.
3. Define Public Revenue.
4. Explain the canons of Taxation.
5. Describe the types of Taxes.

Chapter: 25

Fiscal Policy

25.1 Meaning of Fiscal policy

Fiscal policy is the set of principles and decisions of a government regarding the level of public expenditure and mode of financing them. It is about the effort of government to influence the economy's output, employment and prices by altering the level of public expenditure, taxation and public debt. Arthur Smithies points out, "Fiscal policy is a policy under which the government uses its expenditure and revenue programmes to produce desirable effects and avoid undesirable effects on the national income, production and employment".

25.2 The Importance of Fiscal Policy

The significance of this policy was not at all recognized by economists before the publication of Keynes's General Theory of Employment, Interest and Money. Keynes gave the concept of fiscal policy new meaning and operation of the public finance a new perspective. He made it clear that taxation, public spending and public debt are the effective instruments of public policy capable of determining the level of output and employment. The importance of fiscal policy in modern economies arises from the fact that the State under democracy is called upon to play an active and important role in promoting economic development and providing a vast number of essential public utilities and services like drinking water, sanitation, civic services, primary education, public health, social welfare, defense, etc. Most of these goods are characterized by the property viz. non-marketable; that it cannot be sold in the market to the consumer. But payment has to be regulated in another way, through taxation. In the underdeveloped economies, public finance has to assume yet another role, whereas in developed economies, it aims at maintaining economic stability. In underdeveloped economies, desirous of achieving rapid economic development, the function of public finance is to promote rapid economic development of the country, besides maintaining economic stability.

25.3 Objectives of Fiscal Policy

The principal objectives of fiscal policy in an economy are as follows:

✓ **To mobilize resources for financing the development programmes in the public sector:** Tax policy is to be directed towards effective mobilization of all available resources and to harness them in the execution of development programmes. This implies, on the one hand, diversion of wasteful and luxury spending to saving and on the other hand productive investment of increments that accrue to production as a result of development efforts. Taxation can be a most effective means of increasing the total quantum of savings and investments in any economy where the propensity to consume is normally high.

✓ **To promote development in the private sector:** In a mixed economy, private sector forms an important constituent of the economy. In spite of the growing importance of the public sector in accelerating the process of economic development, the interest of the private sector cannot be neglected. Therefore rebates, reliefs and liberal depreciation allowances may be granted to boost the private sector.

✓ **To bring about an optimum utilization of resources:** The above objective can be achieved through proper allocation of resources. We must direct investment in the desirable channels both in the public and private sectors by providing suitable incentives. Productive resources are, within limits capable of being used in various ways, which may accelerate economic growth. The available resources must find their way into the socially necessary lines of development.

✓ **To restrain inflationary pressures in the economy to ensure economic stability:** The fiscal policy must be used as an instrument for dealing with inflationary or deflationary situations. One way to achieve this is to devise a tax structure, which will automatically counter the economic disturbances as they arise. The second is to make changes in the tax system in order to deal with inflationary or deflationary situations. In countries like India, it is through the direction of the public expenditure rather than taxation that more effective action can be taken to remove the effect of a deflationary spiral. In terms of inflation, anti-inflationary taxes such as excess profit tax and commodity taxes on articles of both general and luxury consumption can be imposed.

✓ **To improve distribution of income and wealth in the community for lessening economic inequalities:** The national income should be properly distributed so that the fruits of development are fairly shared by all people. Equality in income, wealth and opportunities must form an integral part of economic development and social advance. Moreover, redistribution of income in favour of the poorer sections of the society is essential. This can be achieved through taxation. We can also achieve this through an increase in public expenditure for promoting welfare to the less privileged class. Expenditure on agriculture, irrigation, education and health and medical expenses will improve the economic conditions of the weaker sections of the society. Fiscal policy can affect total spending in two ways. The first is the direct change in total spending brought about by the government increasing or decreasing its own expenditure. And the second one is increasing or reducing private spending by varying its own tax revenue.

- ✓ **To obtain full employment and economic growth:** The fiscal policy to achieve full employment and to maintain stable price in the economy has been developed in the recent past. The ineffectiveness of monetary policy as a means to remove unemployment during the Great Depression paved the way for the development of fiscal policy in achieving this objective. For accelerating the rate of growth, allocation of higher proportion of the fully employed resources is needed. Those activities increase the productive capacity of the economy. Therefore fiscal policy is used through its tax instrument to encourage investment and discourage consumption so that production may increase. It is also necessary to increase capital formation by reducing the high income tax on personal income. To increase employment, the state expenditure should be directed towards providing social and economic overheads. The state should undertake local public works of community development involving more labour and less capital per head.

- ✓ **Fiscal policy and capital formation:** Fiscal policy such as taxes, tariffs, transfer payments, rebate and subsidies are expected to spur long run economic growth through increased capital formation. Capital formation is considered an important determinant of economic growth. The economic theory tells us that the optimal amount of capital formation serves a useful key to economic growth in developing economies. At the same time, the economic distortions brought about by lack of adequate fiscal incentives can cause capital formation to fall short of the socially optimal level.

25.4 Limitations of Fiscal Policy

Though the fiscal policy has an important place in economic development and in particular, in the stepping up of saving and investment both in public and in private sectors, it has the following limitations.

- ✓ **Size of fiscal measures:** The budget is not a mere statement of receipts and revenues of the government. It explains and shapes the economic structure of a country. When the budget forms a small part of the national income in developing economies, fiscal policy cannot have the desired impact on the economic development. Direct taxation at times become an instrument of limited applicability, as the vast majority of the people are not covered by it. Further, when the total tax revenue forms a smaller portion of the national income, fiscal measures will not step up the sagging economy requiring massive help.

- ✓ **Fiscal policy as ineffective anti-cyclical measure:** Fiscal measures- both loosening fiscal policy and tightening fiscal policy- will not stimulate speedy economic growth of a country, when the different sectors of the economy are not closely integrated with one another. Action taken by the government may not always have the same effect on all the sectors. Thus we may have for instance the recession in some sectors followed by a rise in prices in other sectors. An increasing purchasing power through deficit financing, a policy advocated by J.M. Keynes in 1930s may not have the effect of reviving the recession hit economies, but merely result in a rise in prices.

✓ **Administrative delay:** Fiscal measures may introduce delay, uncertainties and arbitrariness arising from administrative bottlenecks. As a result, fiscal policy fails to be a powerful and therefore a useful stabilization policy.

Review of Questions

1. What is Fiscal Policy?
2. Explain the importance and objectives of Fiscal Policy.

Chapter: 26

Banking

26.1 Banks

Banks have become the foundation stone of modern economy. It is said to be a financial intermediary. It is in midway between the savers and the users of fund. In simple language, bank refers to an institution which deals in money. Actually bank is a institutions which accepts deposits and makes loans for the purpose of earning profit. There are different types of bank having some common or different functions. Banks may be of various types such Central Bank, commercial banks, development banks, cooperative banks, rural banks etc.

26.2 Commercial Banks

Commercial banks are the most important parts of Banking System. A commercial bank is a financial intermediary and does banking business to earn profit. It takes money from a surplus unit and lends the same fund to a deficit unit at a higher rate of interest. In this way, it makes profit. It is known as a dealer in credit. It may be managed privately or by the Government. The two main functions of these banks are Deposit and Loan function. Deposits are three types: Demand or current, Savings and Fixed or Time deposit. Banks do not lend the entire sum of deposit. But a portion is kept in the form of cash. This is called Cash Reserve Ratio (CRR. In its loans and advances, banks maintain a diversified portfolio in order to seek a balance between liquidity and profitability. Banks perform some other functions that enhance their yield. They keep valuables in their custody, collect chequable amounts, the purchase and sell of shares, debenture. They also act as a agents of their customers.

26.2.1 Functions of Commercial Banks

Commercial banks perform a variety of functions and provide a number of services to their customers. The various functions performed by commercial banks are as follows:

a) Acceptance of Deposits

Commercial Banks accept depots form the public. People who have surplus funds with them would like to deposit these with commercial banks. Banks accept mainly three types of deposits: (i) Current Account, (ii) Savings Account and (iii) Fixed Deposits.

- ✓ **Current Account-** Current account are those accounts in which deposits are payable on demand. They are also known as demand deposits. These accounts are mostly held by traders and businessmen. Banks do not pay any interest on these accounts.

- ✓ **Savings Account-** Saving account are those accounts in which deposits are payable on demand and money can be withdrawn by cheques. Banks impose a limit on the amount and number of withdrawals during a particular period. These accounts are held by households who have idle cash for a short period. Deposits in this account earn interest at nominal rates.

✓ **Fixed Deposits-** Saving account are those accounts in which money is deposited for a fixed period like, 6 months, one year, five years or more. These deposits are not payable on demand. These deposits are also known as time deposits since the money deposited in them cannot be withdrawn before the maturity of the period for which the deposit is made. These are interest-earning deposits. The rate of interest varies with the length of time for which the deposit has been made.

b) Advancing of Loans

Advancing of loans is another function of a commercial bank. Lending is the most profitable business of a bank. Banks charge interest from the borrowers which are more than the interest they pay to their depositors. Now days, Banks advance many types of loans like cash Credit, overdraft, loans and advancing, etc.

✓ **Cash credit-** The entire sanctioned amount of loan by the bank is not given to the borrower at a particular time. The bank opens an account of the borrower and allows him to withdraw the borrowed amount as and when he required the money. The bank charges interest, not on the amount of loan sanctioned, but on the actual amount withdrawn from the bank.

- ✓ **Overdraft-** The customer is allowed to draw cheques in excess of the balance standing to his credit to the extent of the amount of overdraft.

- ✓ **Discounting Bill of Exchange-** Bill of exchange is another method of making advances by the banks. It is drawn by a creditor on the debtor specifying the amount of debt and also the date when it becomes payable. These are normally issued for a period of 90 days. The creditors cannot get it enchased from the debtors before the maturity of the 90 - day's period. If the creditor needs money before the expiry of this 90 day's period, he/ she can get it discounted from a commercial bank. The bank makes payment to the creditor after deducting its commission. When the bill matures, the bank will get payment from the debtor.

c) Credit Creation

A very important and unique function of the commercial banks is to create credit for making profit. In the process of acceptance of deposit and granting of loans, commercial banks are able to create credit. This means that they are able to grant more loans than the amount of initial or primary deposits made by the customers.

d) Transfer of funds

Banks help in the remittance or transfer of funds from one place to another through the use of various credit instruments like cheques, drafts, mail transfers and telegraphic transfers.

e) Facilitation of payments through cheques

Banks have provided a very convenient system of payment in the form of cheques. The cheque is the principal method of payment in business in recent times. It is convenient, cheap and safe means of making payments.

f) Agency Functions

Banks provide various types of agency functions for their customers. The banks charge commission or service charge for these functions. The main agency functions are to collect cheques, drafts, bills of exchange, hundies and other financial Instruments for their customers. They also act as agents for the customers in the sale and purchase of securities.

g) Miscellaneous Services

Commercial banks provide various miscellaneous services, such as provision of locker facilities for safe custody of jewellery and other valuables, issue of travelers cheques, gift cheques, provision of tax assistance and investment advice, etc.

26.3 Principles of Commercial Banks

- ✓ **Principles of liquidity:** Deposits are repayable on demand or after expiry of a certain period. Everyday depositors either deposit or withdraw cash. To meet the demand for cash, all commercial banks have to keep certain amount of cash in their custody.
- ✓ **Principles of profitability:** The driving force of commercial enterprise is to generate profit. So it is true in case of commercial bank also.

- ✓ **Principles of solvency:** Commercial bank should have financially sound and maintain a required capital for running the business.

- ✓ **Principles of safety:** While investing the fund, banks are to be cautions because bank's money is depositor's money.

- ✓ **Principles of collection of savings:** This is a very important principle for today's banking business. Commercial banks always seek huge amount of idle money from the clients. Now a day's banks fix up the target for their employees to generate more savings from the people.

- ✓ **Principles of loan and investment policy:** The main earning sources of commercial banks are lending and investing money to the viable projects. So, commercial banks always try to earn profit through sound investment.

- ✓ **Principles of economy:** Commercial banks never go for any unnecessary expenditure. They always try to maintain their functions with economy that increase their yearly profit.

- ✓ **Principles of providing services:** A better service brings great reputation for the bank.

- ✓ **Principles of secrecy:** Commercial bank maintains and keeps the clients accounts secretly. Nobody except the legitimized person is allowed to see the accounts of the clients.

- ✓ **Principles of modernization:** It is the age of science and technology. So to cope up with the advanced world the commercial bank has to adopt modern technical services like online banking, credit card etc.

✓ **Principles of specialization:** It is an age of specialization. Here commercial banks segments their whole functions into various parts and place their human resources according to their efficiency.

✓ **Principles of location:** Commercial banks choose a suitable site where the availability of customers is large.

✓ **Principles of relation:** Commercial banks always try to maintain a good relation with their clients and potential customers.

✓ **Principles of publicity:** It is an age of publicity. If you would like to earn more money, you have to give more advertisement through various media. In that case, commercial banks follow this kind of principles to increase their customers.

Review of Questions

1. What is Bank?
2. Define Commercial Banks?
3. Define Saving Account.
4. Explain the Principles of Commercial Banks.
5. Describe the functions of Commercial Banks.

Chapter: 27

Central Bank

27.1 Definition of Central Bank

There are no universally accepted definitions of Central Bank because of the functions it discharge. But it may be defined as an institution charged with the responsibility of managing the expansion and contraction of the volume of money supply for general Economic Welfare. In short, Central bank is an Institution that conducts the monetary and banking system of a country. The Central Bank is the apex institution in the banking and financial structure of the country. It is responsible for maintaining the economic stability of a country.

27.2 Distinction between the Central Bank and the Commercial Bank

The Central Bank of a country differs for the commercials Banks in the following manners:

- The Central Bank of a country enjoys supreme monetary authority with wide powers but commercials Banks have no such power to enjoy.
- The Central Bank does not exist to make profits for itself and owners but commercials banks exist and organized for profits their owners.
- Central bank is the ultimate source of money supply to the economy but commercial Banks No such function is performed by it.
- The central bank acts as a banker to the government but commercial Banks acts as a banker to private institutions.
- The central bank is the lender of last resort and hence never fails but commercial Banks often undertakes risky business activities and sometimes may fail.
- The central bank neither does accept deposits from public, nor lends money to the public. But commercial Banks accept deposits and lending money to the public as a most important function.
- The central bank is generally subordinate to the state, i.e. state owned and state managed. But commercial Banks is mostly privately owned and privately managed.
- The central bank issues paper notes in fact it enjoys the monopoly power in this matter. But commercial Banks create credit and cannot issue paper notes.

✓ The basis of cash money issued is gold and foreign reserve for Central bank. Whereas the basis of credit money generated is cash deposit for the commercial banks.

27.3 Functions of Central Bank

Central Bank plays a leading role in supervising, organizing, running, developing and regulating the banking and financial structure of the country. The main functions of the Central bank are as follows:

✓ **Issuing of Note:** The Central Bank enjoys the exclusive right of issuing note in every country of the world. The currency notes issued by the Central Bank are declared unlimited legal tender throughout the country. A large numbers of Central Banks have divided their functions into two departments- Banking Department and Issue Department. It is the Issue Department that is responsible for issuing Note in that country. The Central Bank has also to keep reserve of Gold, Silver and foreign securities for issuing notes.

✓ **Banker, advisor agent to the Government:** All Central banks of the world acts as a Banker, advisor and agent to the government. The Banking accounts of the central and state government are maintained by the Central Bank as the commercial bank does for its customers. As a banker to the government it helps the government in short term loans and advances for temporary requirements. Being a apex bank of the country, it also advise the government from time to time all related matters.

- ✓ **Banker's Bank:** All commercial banks keep some part of their cash balances as deposits with the Central Bank of the country because of convention or legal compulsion. The commercial banks always withdraw currency during the busy season and paying in surplus during the slack season. Part of these balances are meant for clearing purposes i.e.; all commercial banks keep deposit account with the Central Bank. The deposit balances of the Central Bank are considered as cash reserves for general purpose.

- ✓ **Clearing House Facility:** Central Bank also performs the functions of a clearing house. By virtue of its unique position in dealing with domestic and foreign funds the Central Bank has a special position for conducting Clearing house operation, interbank transfer of funds and settlement of accounts. Clearing house facility means providing an opportunity to member commercial banks to settle their claims on each other mutually.

- ✓ **Custodian of Foreign Exchange Reserves for the country:** All central Banks of the world also function as the custodian of the foreign exchange reserve for their respective countries. Under this system the central bank controls both receipts and payments of foreign exchange. A country has in its foreign trade favorable or unfavorable balance. Favorable balance helps to bring foreign exchange to the country while unfavorable balance means paying foreign exchange out. As custodian of Foreign Exchange, Central Bank keeps a constant watch on the same so that the value of the home currency does not rise or fall adversely in relation to foreign currency.

✓ **Control of Credit:** The one of the main function of the Central Bank is to control the credit activities of the commercial banks for the purpose of ensuring price stability and economic growth of a country. The Central Bank ensures price stability and avoids inflationary and deflationary tendencies by several monetary policy methods like regulation of Bank rate, open market operation, change in variable reserve ratio, etc.

23.4 Credit Control

Credit money created by commercial banks and other non-banking financial institutions constitutes a significant portion of total money supply in an economy. Their shortages and excesses may have profound impact upon an economy. The flow of credit should be regulated in such a way that they may raise or fall according to the needs of an economy. This is what we generally means by credit control. This is done by the central bank in its role of a banker's bank. The objective of credit control is generally two fold. A central bank may encourage member banks to expand credit, known as expansionary monetary policy, which is adopted to lift an economy out of depression and unemployment. It may restrict credit-creating power of banks and non-banks which is known as restrictive policy to fight inflation and to achieve financial stability In the context of growth with stability a central bank is to deal with both aspects -

increasing credit flow for more investment and, at the same time, restrict flow of credit so that it may not generate inflation.

23.4.1 Methods of Credit Control

All Central Banks of the world possess a number of methods for controlling credit. These are of two types -Quantitative and Qualitative. Quantitative techniques seek to regulate total quantity of credit while qualitative measures affect the availability of credit. The methods of Credit control is given below:

A. Quantitative Methods:

✓ **Bank Rate Policy:** All central banks as a banker's of Banks lend money or rediscounts the bills of commercial banks. The rates of interest charged by the central banks are known as Bank Rate or Discount rate. By manipulating Bank Rate central Bank can regulate the credit creating power of member banks. If Bank rate is raised by the Central Bank, commercial banks are to borrow at a higher cost. The effectiveness of this technique depends on the extent to which commercial banks depend on central bank for loan and rediscounting. If banks can collect funds from other sources at relatively cheaper rate, they need not depend on central bank credit.

✓ **Open market operations:** Open markets operations imply purchase and sale of securities in the stock market. When the central bank appears in the market as a seller of Government securities, people buy such securities by withdrawing money from banks or the banks themselves invest in such securities instead of granting loan to public. In either case the powers of creating credit will be restricted. On the other hand, if central bank buys securities money flows out thus enlarging the cash base of members banks. Credit expansion depends upon external business environment and borrower's attitudes over which banks have no influence.

✓ **Cash Reserve Ratio:** All Commercial banks of a country are also legally bound to keep a portion of their deposits in the form of Cash Reserve to the Central Bank. It is the most liquid asset in their hand and at the same time it is zero earning assets. Naturally by altering the Cash Reserve Ratio, the central bank can expand or reduce the funds bank can lend. In underdeveloped money market this technique is more suitable than Bank Rate policy and open market operations.

B. Qualitative Credit Controls:

All central banks also possess certain techniques by which they can control the direction and distribution of credit according to purpose and areas wise. The purpose of selective controls is the rational allocation of scarce bank credit and its economic utilization for the purpose of preventing speculative activities with the help of bank credit. These techniques are very helpful in a less-developed economy where overall credit restriction may hinder the growth of a country.

✓ **Moral Suasion:** Moral suasion is a qualitative technique. In this, the central bank requests banks to lend more or not to lend in some sectors. There is no legal compulsion behind their acceptance. Generally if a request is not carried out by the member bank, the central bank may take such steps as banks are forced to accept in the form of directional control, prohibiting loans of particular type or giving advice to grant loan to priority sectors.

Review of Questions

1. What is Central Bank?
2. Explain the functions of Central Bank.

Chapter: 28

Financial Institutions

For the growth and development of any country, financial institutions are very essential and necessary. These institutions are known as Development Banks as they grant long-term development finance. Their spheres of activity are limited. They are also known as non-bank financial intermediaries as they cannot raise money in the form of demand deposits. They may be managed privately or by the government. They also underwrite or subscribe to shares and debentures of the public limited companies. Besides finance they offer technical and managerial advices.

   ✓ **Industrial Financial Institutions:** These types of financial institutions grant loans and advances to the industries of those countries. They may be free to raise resources from the open market. They can subscribe shares and debentures floated by industrial concerns. They may provide guarantee of loans taken from capital market and deferred payment in respect of imports of capital goods by approved concerns. The can grant loans in foreign currencies.

- ✓ **Industrial Development Banks:** These types of banks are established for the development of all types of industries. They may be managed privately or by the government. Its members may be representatives of public sector banks, other financial institutions and experts from different fields. They works as a central coordinating agency for establishing a harmonious relationship among the term lending agencies. It provides direct finance by granting loan and advances, guarantees loans taken from banks, subscribes or underwrites share, bond, and debentures. Besides it can convert its loans into equity shares of the concerned industry. They also assist in the creation, expansion and modernization of industrial units lying within private sector. They encourage and promote private ownership of industrial investment along with the expansion of investment markets. In modern times, the example of this type of bank is Industrial Bank of India.

- ✓ **Mutual Funds:** Mutual funds and those funds which mobilize the savings of the small investors for making available the benefits of equity investment through indirect holding of securities. They may be managed privately or by the government. In this ways, they occupy a pivotal position in the capital market of any country in mobilizing savings of small investors and channeling into productive investment. These savings provide support to new issue market.

✓ **Export Import Banks:** These banks are a non-bank financial intermediary. Their area of operations is related to foreign trade of that country. They are lead bank in the finance and promotion of exports and imports trade. They provide the facilities of Export Bills Re-discounting, Refinance of suppliers credit, Bulk Import finance, Foreign currency Pre shipment credit, Product equipment finance program, Business Advisory and technical Assistance and etc. The example of this type of bank is Export and Import Bank of India.

✓ **Banks for Agriculture and Rural Development :** These types of banks works as the apex body in the sphere of agriculture and rural credit system. They provide all sorts of reference to cooperatives, commercial banks and also Regional Rural Banks. They also inspects the above three agencies and advises the government thereon. They can advance loans to State Governments to enable them to subscribe to the share capital of cooperative Banks. They also help in prompting research in agriculture and rural development. With this, they undertake evaluation and monitoring projects financed by them. They are responsible for the development operation and coordination relating to rural credit. They may borrow from Union Government or in foreign currency.

✓ **Life Insurance Companies:** They are basically an investment institution. They provide life insurance to its policy holders for emergency fund to guard against any financial misfortune and a way to accumulate funds by the time of retirement from work. They also purchases even when the market is dull (bearish) and prices are low in order to reap the benefit of future price appreciation. The LIC plays an important role in the securities market in India.

✓ **General Insurance Companies:** The General Insurance companies sell insurance service against some forms of risk like loss of physical assets of various kinds from fire or accident and against personal sickness and accident. The insurer just purchases a service and not any financial asset. The companies can invest in the shares and debentures of the corporate sector. They also participate in the underwriting of new issues and in granting term loans to industries.

✓ **Securities and Exchange Board:** Securities and Exchange Board regulate the business in Stock or securities markets, collective investment schemes and Mutual Funds. It also prohibits insider trading insecurities, large acquisition of shares and takeover of companies. The example of this type of institution is Stock Exchange Board of India (SEBI).

✓ **The Asian Development Bank (ADB):** ADB established in December 1966. It is engaged in promoting the socioeconomic progress of its member countries in Asia and Pacific. It is owned by the governments of 37 countries from the region and 16 from outside the region. Its head quarters are in Manila, Philippines. The bank's highest policy making body is the Board of

224

Governors. Bank's activities comprise lending activities, and technical assistance. It makes loans and equity investment for the socioeconomic advancement of its member countries and provides technical assistance for the preparation and execution of development projects, and advisory services. It also promotes investment of private and public capital for development purposes. With this, it provides assistance in coordinating development plans and policies of member countries.

✓ **The International Monetary Fund (IMF):** IMF was established to secure the international monetary cooperation in March, 1947. It provides short term credit and functions as a leading institution in foreign exchange. It grants loans for current transactions and not capital transaction. It also helps for the orderly adjustment of exchange rates and acts as a store house of foreign exchange rates which is likely to improve the balance of payment position of member countries.

✓ **The World Bank:** The World Bank has also established with IMF in 1947. It helps reconstruction of member countries damages due to the Second World War. It facilitates the investment of foreign capital for productive purpose and promotes balanced growth of international trade and to maintain equilibrium in the balance of payment. It also promotes private foreign investment by means of guarantee to loans and investments made by private investors. It advances loans out of its resources when private loans are not sufficient. Thus the bank supplements rather than replace private investment.

Review of Questions

1. What are Financial Institutions?

2. Define Life Insurance Corporation?

3. Define General Insurance Companies.